STRONG
MARRIAGENOW

HAPPILY
EVER AFTER

FREE
Online Marriage
Success Quiz

How to Be Happily Married to the One You *Already* Married

Dana Fillmore, Psy.D., and Amy Barnhart

Have a Sweet Life Books
A Division of Have a Sweet Life, Inc.
1804 Neale Street
San Diego, CA 92103

The anecdotes in this book are based on Dr. Dana Fillmore's experience in working with couples. Names and identifying information have been changed. The information contained in this book is intended to be educational and not for diagnosis, prescription, or treatment of any health disorder whatsoever. This information should not replace consultation with a competent health professional. The author and publisher are in no way liable for any misuse of the material.

StrongMarriageNow System ® and Marriage Success Skill ® and Marriage Success System ® are registered trademarks of Have a Sweet Life, Inc.

Cover designed by Budi Setiawan

ISBN-13: 978-0615544465 (Have a Sweet Life, Inc.)

ISBN-10: 0615544460

This book is dedicated to
our wonderful husbands:

Ossie and Kevin

Thank you for your
love, support, and endless patience!

Table of Contents

 # Foreword

Hello! I'm Amy Barnhart and I'm the CEO of StrongMarriageNow.com, a subsidiary of Have a Sweet Life, Inc. I am so excited that you have picked up this book and have taken the first step toward transforming your marriage.

I started StrongMarriageNow.com because I wanted more people to get the benefit of Dr. Dana's advice. Why am I so passionate about sharing her advice with the world? Well, my passion is fueled by my personal experiences. I grew up surrounded by failed marriages. Between my mother, father, brother and two sisters, 13 out of 14 marriages ended in divorce. I watched my family members marry and engage in the same problems over and over again. I personally felt and witnessed the pain of so many broken relationships and vowed that when I married, I would not follow in the footsteps of my family. I committed to staying married and learning what I needed to know to be happy in my marriage. Thankfully, I found Dr.

Dana and decided to partner with her to spread her Marriage Success Skills to the general public so that more people could break out of the patterns my family and so many others fall into. I'm committed to helping others avoid the pain I witnessed and experienced growing up.

Dr. Dana is the ideal person to teach couples how to be happily married because she has been practicing for more than 15 years, has an outstanding success rate and is considered America's Leading Authority on Marriage Success. Three out of four couples report that they want to stay together, not just that they will stay together, but they WANT to stay together after applying her Marriage Success Skills. Recent research studies show that the traditional marriage counseling success rate is less than one out of four!

> To find out if your marriage has what it takes to succeed in the long-term,
> take our Marriage Success Quiz:
> http://strongmarriagenow.com/successquiz

Upon recognizing that so many people would like to work on their marriage, but feel they can't - either because they can't get their partner to go to a counselor or because they simply don't have the time or the money - Dr. Dana and I decided to create the **Marriage Success System** that includes the key skills and concepts she teaches every day in her Clinical Psychology practice. The **Marriage Success System** is designed for people looking for an alternative to face-to-face marriage counseling. This System has been shown to quickly and dramatically impact marriages.

We surveyed hundreds of couples and found their top marriage concerns were: Time Together, Communication, Sex and Money. Therefore, we have written predominantly about these topics, (as well as a few others). We also learned that many couples make critical mistakes in *how* they work on their marriage. They spend most of their time complaining, blaming and shaming each other and focusing mostly on their problems, often times *with* the help and guidance of a marriage counselor! Unfortunately, those efforts only contribute to weakening the relationship even further. What they really need is a step-by-step, proven system that will teach them the practical skills they need to have the marriage of their dreams!

> If you wanted to learn how to swim, you wouldn't just keep hoping and drowning, you'd take swimming lessons!

We set out to create a product that both members of a couple would find helpful and that would put them on the right track. I'm happy to say that both our female *and* male customers find the advice incredibly valuable.

I also want to share that I am a professional business-woman and a mother of two. I've been married for 20 years and my husband and I regularly apply Dr. Dana's advice to our marriage. My husband especially likes Dr. Dana's *balanced* perspective and how quickly he can get answers.

These topics are not about men becoming more like women. He feels he doesn't have to rifle through "a lot of fluff" to get quick, valuable information that really makes an immediate difference. Instead, he gets clear, practical steps he can easily apply.

In many ways, my husband and I are more in love now than when we first met! I am pleased to say the **Marriage Success System** really works. I am thrilled to be sharing Dr. Dana's advice with you and am committed to making this valuable information available to people around the world. I wish you a happy, loving, and STRONG MARRIAGE NOW!

Amy Barnhart
President & CEO
Have a Sweet Life, Inc.

Get 3 FREE Marriage Success Secrets from Dr. Dana. You'll discover:
- The marriage truth no one ever told you
- The secret of happily married couples
- How to make everything easier in your relationship
- How to end the fighting
- Tips to improve your sex life
... and many more
Sign up today at:
http://strongmarriagenow.com/secrets

Section I

Getting Started

In this section, you will learn:

- All About Dr. Dana Fillmore
- How the **Marriage Success System** can dramatically improve your marriage.
- How the System works
- What you need to do to get the most out of it

Before you get started with the System, we encourage each of you to take a moment to complete **Exercise A: What Brought You Together.** **(Two copies have been provided for your convenience: A1, A2)**

Exercise A1: What Brought You Together?

Step 1: Gather and display photos of yourself and your partner from early in your relationship. Remember that you chose your partner for a reason. Try to get back in touch with those feelings.

Step 2: Write the story of how you and your spouse met and how you knew when you were in love. *(Feel free to write elsewhere, if not enough space provided below.)*

_____

_____

_____

_____

_____

_____

_____

Step 3: List the top three things that attracted you to your spouse

1. _____

2. _____

3. _____

Step 4: List their three best qualities today

1. _____

2. _____

3. _____

Exercise A2: What Brought You Together?

Step 1: Gather and display photos of yourself and your partner from early in your relationship. Remember that you chose your partner for a reason. Try to get back in touch with those feelings.

Step 2: Write the story of how you and your spouse met and how you knew when you were in love. *(Feel free to write elsewhere, if not enough space provided below.)*

_____

_____

_____

_____

_____

_____

_____

Step 3: List the top three things that attracted you to your spouse

1. _____

2. _____

3. _____

Step 4: List their three best qualities today

1. _____

2. _____

3. _____

 **Chapter 1**

Introduction

In this chapter, you'll learn to:

- Agree on ground rules for working together during this process
- Remember why you chose each other in the first place
- Clarify what each of you wants from your relationship
- Take steps to start improving your marriage right away

Congratulations on investing in your marriage!

I'm Dr. Dana Fillmore. I have a Masters and a Doctorate degree in Psychology and I have been in practice for over 15 years in San Diego, California. My practice focuses primarily on couples and families. I utilize the principles of Cognitive-Behavioral Therapy. This approach focuses on the "here and now" by using a goal-oriented systematic approach in order to more quickly solve problems. The basic underlying principles are based on the premise that our thoughts affect our feelings and our feelings affect how we act. This means, that if we change our thoughts, we can change how we feel and how we act.

All the concepts written about here are based on both current research and my clinical experience. These are the skills that I teach couples over months of once-a-week sessions.

> **Note:** In the interest of simplicity and for the purposes of this book, I have chosen to use the terms, husband, wife, spouse, and marriage but these principles can be applied to any loving relationship.

On a personal note, I am a working wife and mother of two young children. I know exactly how hard it is to try and balance everything in one's life! But, because my husband and I try to use the very skills described here, we've been happily married for over 17 years.

There's a System
That Can Help!

There is a reason that most couples come to therapy for one hour once a week. It takes time and practice to apply new skills. Actually, research suggests that it takes 21 days of practicing a new behavior to create a new habit.

Consequently, I have developed the **Marriage Success System** to guide you through, step-by-step. It includes:

- Information on Marriage Success skills and concepts
- Exercises to help build skills and knowledge. Where relevant, we've included two copies of the exercise - one for each partner – just as with exercise A1 and A2
- Straightforward, specific tasks to do each week to improve your marriage
- *"To-Do's"* and *"Commitments"* to reinforce what you're learning

Following the **Marriage Success System** only takes an average of fifteen minutes a day. And it will help you develop new habits and dramatically improve your relationship. There is also a companion video course to the System at www.StrongMarriageNow.com that I highly recommend as well.

Get a sample of the companion video course as well as 3 FREE Marriage Success Secrets from Dr. Dana. You'll discover:

- The marriage truth no one ever told you
- The secret of happily married couples
- How to make everything easier in your relationship
- How to end the fighting
- Tips to improve your sex life

... and many more

Sign up today at:

http://strongmarriagenow.com/secrets

Many couples have found it easier to get their spouse to learn and apply these skills by watching these videos rather than by reading about them. If you find you're in this situation, you may want to check out the online video course!

If you are currently reading this by yourself, that's okay! It can still have a major impact on your marriage, even if you're the only one working on the relationship. If you do want to get your partner to participate and you're not sure how, you might want to point out that you have found something that you not only think *both* of you can learn from, but that *both* of you can benefit from as well.

If you still feel like you'd like to get your spouse involved, check out our special 2-part video course entitled "How to Get Your Partner Checked Back Into Your Marriage:" http://strongmarriagenow.com/checkin

Ideally, most of these chapters are designed for you and your spouse to review together. Additionally, there are a few sections that are tailored for each of you separately. To get the most out of the course, I suggest that each of you read a section together, complete the exercises, practice the skills, (the "*To-Do*" Lists), and then revisit the chapter if you feel the need to fine-tune.

Understand that it takes time to grow and adapt to new skill-sets. Have patience with yourself and your partner during this process, but stick with it! Your relationship with the person you love is worth the effort!

Avoid a Common Mistake

Now, let me tell you about a common mistake that couples make when they come into therapy. After the first couple of sessions, their marriage improves somewhat and the combination of the cost, the inconvenience and frankly, the pain associated with tackling these tough issues causes them to stop coming to therapy. This can be a big mistake. Couples therapy is like tuning up your car; if there's engine trouble, you won't fix it by simply changing the spark plugs! The fact is, like anything complicated, there are a lot of important parts that require attention. Consequently, I recommend following the **Marriage Success System** and reading **all** of the chapters, whether you feel they apply to you or not.

Going through this material will likely bring up issues in your marriage that need to be dealt with sooner rather than later. But I tell couples, working on your marriage is like exercising in a gym; it can really hurt while you are doing it, but you feel much better and stronger afterward.

A Common Misconception

People can't change! We hear it all the time, right? Wrong.

The belief that people never change is completely untrue; in fact the opposite is true. People change *all* the time. It's actually the one thing we can count on in life. Most of you wouldn't be reading this book if one or both of you hadn't changed; changed how you feel about each other, changed what you wanted out of life, changed how you treat each other. People change throughout their entire lives. The question is how motivated are you to change for the better? And do you know how?

It's important to learn how to make positive changes in your life, because a couple who is capable of adapting and growing and changing can weather almost all life throws at them.

Now, I want to tell you the difference between people who stay married and those who don't stay married. The people who stay married are willing to work on it. They're willing to change, to learn, to grow, to take risks and to take action. Basically, they're willing to do whatever it takes! I encourage you to ask yourself, "Am I someone who is willing to work on my marriage?" "Am I willing to consider change?" If so, you're well on your way to an amazing marriage!

The second part of this misconception is that while people may change, they quickly go back to their old habits. This can be true, but only if they don't learn a new way to do things and put those new skills into action. That's exactly why we created the **Marriage Success System** so that you can learn and apply essential relationship skills to give you the marriage you really want.

Don't Worry, It's Normal

Finally, I need to tell you this – falling in and out of love in a long-term marriage is perfectly normal. We did not stand up before God and Man, (and most of our friends and relatives), and make promises for only those times when we are madly in love. Instead, we made a commitment to get us through those times when we want to toss our partners through the nearest window. Have you ever noticed it's "Sickness" first and then "Health?" Till "Death do us part" – There's a point to that!

The truth is, all marriages have their ups and downs, their good times and bad. Nevertheless, research indicates that 86% of underlinehappily married couples that stay together and *work* on their marriage report being much happier later on in life. Further, when couples give up on their marriage and subsequently divorce, it often creates a significant impact on not only the individuals in the marriage, but also the children. Research suggests that children of divorced parents often have lower self-esteem, higher incidence of drug and alcohol use, increased behavioral problems, lower grades, increased suicide rates and many may have significant difficulties later in relationships of their own.

And those are just the couples that are simply considering the impact on the children. I'm also amazed by how many people think that *their* lives will get simpler if they get divorced. They fail to comprehend the impact of this kind of decision: significantly decreased financial resources, the pain and inconvenience of shared custody, dealing with new spouses and maybe even step-children, giving up half the power and control over how their own kids are being raised, (not to mention half of the time!) and many people actually don't anticipate the possibility that they could spend the rest of their life alone.

And did you know that a divorced person's life span can actually be shortened? These are all things to think about when considering whether to give up on or work on your marriage.

This System Is Not for Everyone

I want to be clear. This book is pro-marriage. Having said that, there are families experiencing problems that are bigger than the scope of this book; *e.g.* problems involving severe substance abuse, physical, sexual and emotional abuse, and many dangerous mental health disorders. If **any** of these are occurring in your marriage, I strongly encourage you to seek professional help *immediately*.

Ground Rules

Now, if you believe the **Marriage Success System** is right for you and you're ready to get started, let's cover some ground rules. These will help you and your spouse work together to create positive change:

1. **<u>Don't</u> blame!** This material is not meant to be a hammer that you use to beat your partner over the head. In fact, blaming is one of the most common mistakes that couples make when "working" on their marriage. They focus primarily on what the other person is doing wrong and take little to no responsibility for their part in the couple's problems or issues. Focusing on blame only drives you and your spouse further apart. Instead, use this System to look for solutions: new behaviors and positive choices.

2. **<u>Don't</u> "nag" each other!** While going through the book, if you note something you believe applies to your partner – do not say, "See! (Implied here is, 'You idiot!'), That's *exactly* what I've been saying all along! Why haven't you listened to me?" Instead, let the **System** work. It's designed to shine a neutral light on each person's contribution to the problems in the relationship and provide insight into what each person can personally do to change.

3. **<u>Do</u> have loving discussions** - and by that I do not mean, holding hands and singing "Kum-by-yah"

together – instead, I mean: be honest, open and (gulp), vulnerable. Understanding that this may be incredibly difficult for couples that are hurting, we've dedicated two whole sections of the book to learning how to have loving productive discussions, (see Section 3: Understanding Each Other and Section 4: Resolving Conflict).

4. **<u>Do</u> have the courage to talk about what's** *really* **going on with you in your marriage.** For example: When you are frustrated and hurt that your partner is working long hours and paying very little time and attention to you and the kids, he or she won't understand what is *really* going on with you if you criticize them for never making dinner, disapprove of their "improper" technique when putting the kids to bed or complain about the lack of sex. These complaints won't let them know what's *really* going on. Instead, take the time to self-reflect and determine what you are <u>really</u> feeling and what is <u>really</u> causing it. Then kindly, lovingly and *<u>without blame</u>*, discuss your feelings with your spouse.

Following these ground rules as you read this book and completing the **Marriage Success System** will make the experience of working on your relationship go much more smoothly.

Get the Most Out of the System

I don't know how many people over the years have come into my office and said, "This, (meaning couples therapy), isn't working." Inevitably I ask them, "Did you change this thing I suggested?" "Well, no." "Did you do that thing I asked you to do? "Well, not really." Did you take those steps we talked about? "Umm, not yet." The **Marriage Success System**, like therapy, only works if you follow the advice and actually take steps to change your life. Consequently, if you truly desire to see dramatic change in your marriage, I strongly recommend that you read the entire book, complete all of the exercises and take action on the *To-Do's* for each section. I also encourage you to sign up for our 3 free Marriage Success Secrets at www.StrongMarriageNow.com/secrets as we offer ongoing marriage advice that you may find helpful.

It's Worth It!

If you can remember that there was once a time when you were in love with your partner enough to walk down, (or stand waiting at the end of), an aisle and promise forever, then it is absolutely worth it to read this book and do the work. I know if you put in the time, follow the **Marriage Success System**, learn and use these skills, you **will** have the wonderful marriage you desire. I wish you the very best!

Dana Fillmore, Psy.D.
Clinical and Consulting Psychologist
and Co-Founder of **StrongMarriageNow.com**

Exercise B1: What Kind of Marriage Do You Want to Build?

This exercise will help you, as an individual, visualize the marriage you want to have, help you get in touch with the relationship you're wishing for, and get a clear picture of the marriage you're striving to build. As you review the list, take the time to visualize each characteristic in your mind and feel what it would be like to experience these qualities in your life. We recommend that you do not discuss this with your spouse, initially. At the end of the exercise, please simply exchange lists.

Step 1: How important are each of these qualities *to you* in your marriage?

	Not Important ------Essential				
Effective Communication	1	2	3	4	5
(*Understand each other,* *Can resolve conflict*)					
Praise and Appreciation	1	2	3	4	5
Financial Security	1	2	3	4	5
Agreement on Parenting	1	2	3	4	5
Fun and Excitement	1	2	3	4	5
Division of Labor/Chores (*Fairness*)	1	2	3	4	5
Spiritual/Religious Compatibility	1	2	3	4	5
Common Life Goals	1	2	3	4	5
Satisfying Sex Life	1	2	3	4	5
Shared Interests	1	2	3	4	5
Physical Affection	1	2	3	4	5
Strong friendship (*Like each other?*)	1	2	3	4	5
Dependability /Responsibility	1	2	3	4	5
Trust (*Honesty/Commitment*)	1	2	3	4	5
Mutual Respect	1	2	3	4	5
Courtesy, Consideration (*Not Nagging, Criticizing or Shaming*)	1	2	3	4	5
Emotional Support	1	2	3	4	5
Management of Anger	1	2	3	4	5
Acceptance of "real" you	1	2	3	4	5
Agreement on Extended Family Interactions	1	2	3	4	5

Step 2: How important do you believe these qualities are *to your spouse*? (Don't discuss this with your spouse now. You'll exchange later)

	Not Important ------Essential				
Effective Communication	1	2	3	4	5
(Understand each other,					
Can resolve conflict)					
Praise and Appreciation	1	2	3	4	5
Financial Security	1	2	3	4	5
Agreement on Parenting	1	2	3	4	5
Fun and Excitement	1	2	3	4	5
Division of Labor/Chores	1	2	3	4	5
(Fairness)					
Spiritual/Religious	1	2	3	4	5
Compatibility					
Common Life Goals	1	2	3	4	5
Satisfying Sex Life	1	2	3	4	5
Shared Interests	1	2	3	4	5
Physical Affection	1	2	3	4	5
Strong friendship	1	2	3	4	5
(Like each other?)					
Dependability	1	2	3	4	5
/Responsibility					
Trust	1	2	3	4	5
(Honesty/Commitment)					
Mutual Respect	1	2	3	4	5
Courtesy, Consideration	1	2	3	4	5
(Not Nagging, Criticizing					
or Shaming)					
Emotional Support	1	2	3	4	5
Management of Anger	1	2	3	4	5
Acceptance of "real" you	1	2	3	4	5
Agreement on Extended	1	2	3	4	5
Family Interactions					

Step 3: What do you think your marriage looks like now? Rank how satisfied you are with these qualities in your marriage today:

	Not Important ------Essential				
Effective Communication *(Understand each other, Can resolve conflict)*	1	2	3	4	5
Praise and Appreciation	1	2	3	4	5
Financial Security	1	2	3	4	5
Agreement on Parenting	1	2	3	4	5
Fun and Excitement	1	2	3	4	5
Division of Labor/Chores *(Fairness)*	1	2	3	4	5
Spiritual/Religious Compatibllity	1	2	3	4	5
Common Life Goals	1	2	3	4	5
Satisfying Sex Life	1	2	3	4	5
Shared Interests	1	2	3	4	5
Physical Affection	1	2	3	4	5
Strong friendship *(Like each other?)*	1	2	3	4	5
Dependability /Responsibility	1	2	3	4	5
Trust *(Honesty/Commitment)*	1	2	3	4	5
Mutual Respect	1	2	3	4	5
Courtesy, Consideration *(Not Nagging, Criticizing or Shaming)*	1	2	3	4	5
Emotional Support	1	2	3	4	5
Management of Anger	1	2	3	4	5
Acceptance of "real" you	1	2	3	4	5
Agreement on Extended Family Interactions	1	2	3	4	5

Step 4: Circle your top three priorities to improve (from the list in Step 3)

Step 5: Now, exchange your list with your spouse
The point of this exercise is to simply note what is most important to each of you. I recommend that you do not discuss, debate or argue as it is meant solely for the purpose of determining what each of you want your marriage to look like <u>after</u> completing the **Marriage Success System**. Rest assured, the system provides you with the tools needed to help you transform your marriage!

If you'd like another way to determine which
areas of your marriage to focus on,
take our Marriage Success Quiz
http://strongmarriagenow.com/successquiz

Exercise B2: What Kind of Marriage Do You Want to Build?

This exercise will help you, as an individual, visualize the marriage you want to have, help you get in touch with the relationship you're wishing for, and get a clear picture of the marriage you're striving to build. As you review the list, take the time to visualize each characteristic in your mind and feel what it would be like to experience these qualities in your life. We recommend that you do not discuss this with your spouse, initially. At the end of the exercise, please simply exchange lists.

Step 1: How important are each of these qualities *to you* in your marriage?

	Not Important ------Essential				
Effective Communication	1	2	3	4	5
(Understand each other,					
Can resolve conflict)					
Praise and Appreciation	1	2	3	4	5
Financial Security	1	2	3	4	5
Agreement on Parenting	1	2	3	4	5
Fun and Excitement	1	2	3	4	5
Division of Labor/Chores	1	2	3	4	5
(Fairness)					
Spiritual/Religious	1	2	3	4	5
Compatibility					
Common Life Goals	1	2	3	4	5
Satisfying Sex Life	1	2	3	4	5
Shared Interests	1	2	3	4	5
Physical Affection	1	2	3	4	5
Strong friendship	1	2	3	4	5
(Like each other?)					
Dependability	1	2	3	4	5
/Responsibility					
Trust	1	2	3	4	5
(Honesty/Commitment)					
Mutual Respect	1	2	3	4	5
Courtesy, Consideration	1	2	3	4	5
(Not Nagging, Criticizing					
or Shaming)					
Emotional Support	1	2	3	4	5
Management of Anger	1	2	3	4	5
Acceptance of "real" you	1	2	3	4	5
Agreement on Extended	1	2	3	4	5
Family Interactions					

Step 2: How important do you believe these qualities are *to your spouse*? (Don't discuss this with your spouse now. You'll exchange later)

	Not Important ------Essential				
Effective Communication *(Understand each other, Can resolve conflict)*	1	2	3	4	5
Praise and Appreciation	1	2	3	4	5
Financial Security	1	2	3	4	5
Agreement on Parenting	1	2	3	4	5
Fun and Excitement	1	2	3	4	5
Division of Labor/Chores *(Fairness)*	1	2	3	4	5
Spiritual/Religious Compatibility	1	2	3	4	5
Common Life Goals	1	2	3	4	5
Satisfying Sex Life	1	2	3	4	5
Shared Interests	1	2	3	4	5
Physical Affection	1	2	3	4	5
Strong friendship *(Like each other?)*	1	2	3	4	5
Dependability /Responsibility	1	2	3	4	5
Trust *(Honesty/Commitment)*	1	2	3	4	5
Mutual Respect	1	2	3	4	5
Courtesy, Consideration *(Not Nagging, Criticizing or Shaming)*	1	2	3	4	5
Emotional Support	1	2	3	4	5
Management of Anger	1	2	3	4	5
Acceptance of "real" you	1	2	3	4	5
Agreement on Extended Family Interactions	1	2	3	4	5

Step 3: What do you think your marriage looks like now? Rank how satisfied you are with these qualities in your marriage today:

	Not Important			------Essential	
Effective Communication *(Understand each other, Can resolve conflict)*	1	2	3	4	5
Praise and Appreciation	1	2	3	4	5
Financial Security	1	2	3	4	5
Agreement on Parenting	1	2	3	4	5
Fun and Excitement	1	2	3	4	5
Division of Labor/Chores *(Fairness)*	1	2	3	4	5
Spiritual/Religious Compatibility	1	2	3	4	5
Common Life Goals	1	2	3	4	5
Satisfying Sex Life	1	2	3	4	5
Shared Interests	1	2	3	4	5
Physical Affection	1	2	3	4	5
Strong friendship *(Like each other?)*	1	2	3	4	5
Dependability /Responsibility	1	2	3	4	5
Trust *(Honesty/Commitment)*	1	2	3	4	5
Mutual Respect	1	2	3	4	5
Courtesy, Consideration *(Not Nagging, Criticizing or Shaming)*	1	2	3	4	5
Emotional Support	1	2	3	4	5
Management of Anger	1	2	3	4	5
Acceptance of "real" you	1	2	3	4	5
Agreement on Extended Family Interactions	1	2	3	4	5

Step 4: Circle your top three priorities to improve (from the list in Step 3)

Step 5: Now, exchange your list with your spouse

The point of this exercise is to simply note what is most important to each of you. I recommend that you do not discuss, debate or argue as it is meant solely for the purpose of determining what each of you want your marriage to look like <u>after</u> completing the **Marriage Success System**. Rest assured, the system provides you with the tools needed to help you transform your marriage!

If you'd like another way to determine which
areas of your marriage to focus on,
take our Marriage Success Quiz
http://strongmarriagenow.com/successquiz

What You Need To Know

1. It will take time to practice the skills. Pace yourself and follow the System.

2. If you're doing this alone, don't worry. Even one spouse completing the **Marriage Success System** can make a big difference in your relationship.

3. You can't tune-up your car just by changing the spark plugs. - Read *all* of the chapters in the book.

4. Follow the ground rules:

   a. Don't blame
   b. Don't "nag" (criticize/attack) each other
   c. Do have loving discussions
   d. Do talk about what's really going on

5. All marriages have their ups and downs. Stick with it! Most people who stay and work on their marriage are much happier later.

6. There is a reason you married him/her in the first place. Get back in touch with what you *loved* about the person with whom you first fell in *love*.

7. You have to *know* what you really want in your marriage in order to *create* what you really want in your marriage.

What You Can Do To Get Started

Here are the **Marriage Success System** *To-Do's* to Get Started:

1. **Commit** to follow the **Marriage Success System** (complete agreement below).
2. Post the **To-Do** list on your refrigerator, bathroom mirror and in your car and **review** it every day.
3. **Tell, text or email** your partner every day at least one thing that you appreciate about him/her.
4. Note one of your partner's top marriage priorities (review Exercise B) and go out of your way to work toward meeting that need.

For your convenience, we have provided Commitment Cards that include the **Marriage Success System** *To-Do's.*

Be sure to go to Appendix B, cut out your Commitment Cards and post them where each of you will see them every day.

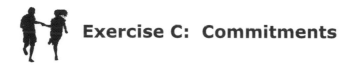 **Exercise C: Commitments**

Fill in your name and sign below. If you're both working on this, have each partner sign his/her own commitment line.

I, _____ , *commit to following the* **Marriage Success System**. *I will follow the relationship ground rules, watch the videos, practice the skills, complete the exercises and accomplish my To-Do's every week. By doing so, I plan to see an immediate and dramatic improvement in my marriage.*

Signed,

_____

I, _____, *commit to following the* **Marriage Success System**. *I will follow the relationship ground rules, watch the videos, practice the skills, complete the exercises and accomplish my To-Do's every week. By doing so, I plan to see an immediate and dramatic improvement in my marriage.*

Signed,

Section II

Spending Time Together

In this section, you will learn:

- The Secret of Happily Married Couples
- The *Most Important Lesson*
- How to better manage your priorities and balance your life
- How to "Make the Time"
- How to plan your Together Activities

Chapter 2

Time – The Most Important Lesson

In this chapter, you will learn:

- What every couple needs to know
- How to think about priorities
- How to prevent an affair
- How to stay deeply in love

Time Alone Together
is Essential

What do you imagine is the single most important commodity in a marriage? (No, it is not more sleep.) It's Time; and by Time, I mean **Time Alone Together**. This is one of the most important lessons couples need to learn; it is also the lesson that *most* couples struggle with every day. Putting this lesson into action supports <u>everything</u> else, from communication, showing affection, and sex, to making your marriage fun and exciting and most of all, to making it work!

The average couple can spend as little as one hour alone together per week; the average couple with kids – sometimes none. The average two people having an affair spend at least 15 hours per week together! Think about that for a moment. Those two people somehow manage to find 15 hours together in spite of all their other commitments, (which often include other spouses and children, etc.). When I work with couples, I ask them to find a mere 8 hours a week for each other. They frequently tell me how difficult this is for them. If you feel the same way, don't worry, we explain exactly how to find the time in Chapter 3: Make the Time.

Make Sure You're Growing Together, Not Apart

Remember when you were first together and you couldn't get enough of each other? You spent hours talking and laughing, learning about each other, what you cared about, what your dreams were, what your fears were, what you liked about each other? What most people don't realize is those things continue to grow and change over time and if we're not checking in and spending time **with** each other, we are, by definition, growing **away** from each other and potentially growing apart.

I don't know how many couples have come to me over the years on the verge of divorce, that tell me there are no major issues, but they've just "grown apart." What "grown apart" tells me is that they have not been spending enough time together. If you do not continue to connect throughout your married life, you run the risk of being married to a stranger. The reality is, it is virtually impossible to be in love with someone you don't *really* know and are not connected with; and it is virtually impossible to truly know someone with whom you never spend time; you can certainly "love" them – but be "in love"? No. There's a reason why 90% of long distance relationships fail within a year. They simply don't spend enough time together. Further, as we've already mentioned, couples that don't spend enough time alone together **can't** meet each other's emotional needs and as such, one or both may be tempted into an affair. If you're not meeting each other's needs, chances greatly increase that one or both of you may be more easily tempted to find someone else who will.

Time Makes
Everything Else Easier

Of course there are other critical components in a happy, healthy marriage, like communication and affection, to name just a few. But how can you work on communication, if you never have the time to talk to each other? How can you work on affection if you don't spend time together? How can you resolve money issues if you're rarely in the same room? How can you learn to be a team, if you're always alone?

I can explain, in great detail about all of these topics, but unless *you* take the time to be alone to talk with each other, to be affectionate with one another and to enjoy each other, you've lost the single most vital component in any marriage and things can only begin to crumble.

The relationship you build and maintain between the two of you is the foundation of the marriage and the family. If you don't take the time, you don't have a relationship. If you don't have a relationship, the family suffers. It bears repeating: It is virtually impossible to have a happy, healthy marriage without *regularly* spending enough time alone together.

We Must Spend Time Together as a "Man" and a "Woman"

When we're married, we spend a lot of time together as husband and wife with friends and family, paying bills, taking care of the home, interacting as a couple. We also spend a great deal of time as individuals in our separate jobs with separate interests. Many of us spend a lot of our time as a mom and a dad, playing with the kids, enjoying family outings. But most of us spend very little time as a "man" and a "woman" together. This is often at the root of many of the complaints that bring couples to therapy: "We just don't feel connected anymore," or "He doesn't pay enough attention to me," or "She's always mad at me," or "We aren't having enough sex." When I hear these complaints, I know for a fact that these things are happening, in large part, because among their priorities, spending time alone together is usually last on their list.

In order, our priorities should be:

1. Marriage
2. Children
3. Job
4. Family and Friends

To help you assess your priorities and help you get them back in balance, we've created an exercise to follow below.

 **Exercise D1: Balance and Priorities**

This exercise is designed to help you identify the most important areas of your life and help reveal areas in your life that may be out of balance.

1. In no particular order, list the important parts of your life:
   (i.e. marriage, kids, job, hobbies, spirituality, friends, health and exercise, extended family, etc.)

   a. _____

   b. _____

   c. _____

   d. _____

   e. _____

   f. _____

   g. _____

2. Label the sections of the circle below with the top eight most important parts of your life.

3. Draw a line in each pie piece to indicate how satisfied you are with the amount of time you're spending on those parts of your life. If you're completely satisfied, the line is on the outer edge of the circle, if you're unsatisfied, it's near the center.

4. Reflect on how satisfied you are with the important aspects of your life. Is it balanced? Would your wheel roll smoothly?

Exercise D2: Balance and Priorities

This exercise is designed to help you identify the most important areas of your life and help reveal areas in your life that may be out of balance.

1. In no particular order, list the important parts of your life:
   (i.e. marriage, kids, job, hobbies, spirituality, friends, health and exercise, extended family, etc.)

   a. _____

   b. _____

   c. _____

   d. _____

   e. _____

   f. _____

   g. _____

2. Label the sections of the circle below with the top eight most important parts of your life.

3. Draw a line in each pie piece to indicate how satisfied you are with the amount of time you're spending on those parts of your life. If you're completely satisfied, the line is on the outer edge of the circle, if you're unsatisfied, it's near the center.

4. Reflect on how satisfied you are with the important aspects of your life. Is it balanced? Would your wheel roll smoothly?

If The Order Gets Mixed-Up,
Things Inevitably Start to Fall Apart

When I suggest to a couple that they place their priorities in this order (marriage, kids, job, family), most of them look at me like I've lost my mind. "What about my job?" they ask. "I have to work to provide for my family." Here are some stories of couples that struggled with the same issues and successfully resolved them.

REAL LIFE EXAMPLES Bill and Merlene came to my office in designer clothes and explained to me that Bill had "no choice" but to work 60 hours a week and therefore didn't have enough time to spend with his wife. Then I watched them drive away in an $80,000 Mercedes. I've also seen Roy and Joan, who work 3 jobs between them just to pay the rent on their condo. Yet after speaking with them further, I learn that after putting the kids to bed, they watch 2 hours of TV every night because they're "so exhausted."

When I worked with these two couples, I explained that while it is important, of course, to pay the mortgage and the bills, we still need to make every effort to arrange our priorities and our finances in such a way as to accommodate spending a significant amount of time with our spouse. For instance, after counseling, Bill and Merlene reassessed their priorities – they both agreed Bill would work fewer hours, despite the fact that this negatively impacted their finances to some extent, so that they might spend more time together. Roy and Joan had little financial choice but to work such long hours. Nevertheless, they agreed to stop watching television (well, four out of seven nights a week anyway), and found they had much more time (and energy!) to spend just "hanging out," playing games together, laughing, talking and enjoying one another.

While in completely different situations, both of these couples struggled with the same issue. Regardless of one's financial status, workload, family responsibilities, etc. they learned that it's essential to invest the time in their marriage.

By doing so, Merlene and Bill and Roy and Joan found that they were more connected, enjoyed each other again and were therefore ready to take on some of the other challenging issues in their marriage.

Your Marriage is the Foundation and Must Come First

Another point often raised involves the children; "I love my spouse, but I don't get to see my kids all week. I can only spend time with them at night and on the weekends!"

REAL LIFE EXAMPLE

I've seen Renee and Jack, a couple with three young children. He works long hours for a start-up company; she is a stay-at-home mom who is very involved in the school's PTA, organizes the local car-pool, participates in the neighborhood playgroup every Friday night and who teaches Sunday school every week on top of her every day responsibilities in the home. They both adore their kids, but because Jack works so many long hours, he understandably wants to spend as much time as possible with the kids when he can.

I explained to Renee and Jack that I understood what it meant to be a working couple with children. However, I had to gently point out that if the marriage fell apart, it *all* fell apart. I explained that their kids would not thank them if they put them before the marriage only to end up getting a divorce. Initially this was hard for them to accept, but I explained that putting one's spouse first is the **most** valuable component in strengthening the marriage.

Renee and Jack got the picture and got their priorities back on track. They began utilizing a written schedule, (covered in the next Chapter: Make The Time), and always started with the question, "When will we spend time alone together this week?" After that question was answered, they were able to schedule the rest of the time with kids, work, and other activities. Once Jack realized that they could put their marriage first and still have quality time with the family, he was happily willing to commit the time, which resulted in significantly strengthening their marriage.

It's All Easier When
You Have Regular Dates

I have worked with many couples and I've asked them to do many things to save their marriages. Yet, I have noted that it is easier to get people to sell their homes or quit their jobs than it is to get them to go on a regular date!

REAL LIFE EXAMPLE

For instance, I worked with Joel and Diana for several months. As usual, we discussed the "Time" issue at the very beginning of our sessions together and they acknowledged that they spent very little time together. Over the next several weeks, we worked on their communication with each other, their sex life, his anger issues and their constant fighting over money. A few issues improved but overall, they remained stuck. Every week I'd ask, "How was date night?" They would laugh, look a little guilty and reply, "We just can't seem to find the time." After a particularly tense session when Joel complained yet again about their lack of sexual activity, I asked them, (rather vehemently), one more time. "Did you pay any attention to each other this week? What did *you*, Joel, do to make her feel connected to you? What did *you*, Diana, do to make him feel appreciated this week? And *when* did you do it!! You don't spend any time together!!"

They finally got the message and began spending time alone together, primarily by scheduling regular dates. When they did, everything we had talked about over the past couple of months just clicked. Their relationship improved greatly thereafter. I see this pattern in the couples I work with time and time again.

Schedule at least 8 Hours Per Week of Time Alone Together

Today, I am asking you to get out your calendars and schedule at least 8 hours per week of **Time Alone Together** with your spouse. Do it!

Remember – if you have any other questions, sign up for our ongoing advice and support at StrongMarriageNow.com today!

What You Need To Know

1. Spending at least **8 hours** a week of quality time alone together makes everything easier in your marriage.

2. The relationship between the two of you is the foundation of the marriage and family. If you two don't have a meaningful relationship, everything else suffers.

3. We must spend time connecting as a **Man and a Woman**, (not just as Mom & Dad and Husband & Wife).

4. In order, our priorities should always be: **Marriage, Kids, Job, Family & Friends**, etc.

Chapter 3

Make the Time

In this chapter, you will learn:

- About Alone Time - What it is and isn't
- How to connect
- How to find the time
- How to have a more comfortable, easy marriage

What Alone Time Is and Isn't

What is Time Alone Together? Well, first, I'm going to describe what it is *not*: It is not watching TV together, not going to a movie together, not going to a loud bar together, not reading your own books in bed while lying next to each other, (not even describing the good parts to each other!) and it is not being in one room together while the kids are awake and in another. Also, it is not being in the same room together while you're on Facebook! (Welcome to the 21st century.) Additionally, time alone together is *not* going out with other couples, though it is very important to have close friends that support the marriage. And finally, it is *not* spending time together along with the family, (kids, in-laws, etc.). Despite the fact that this is the second most important priority – it doesn't count as **Time Alone Together**.

Time alone together must be in a place where you can make eye contact and talk *only* with each other for a significant block of uninterrupted time. It occurs anywhere you feel like you can let your guard down and connect. This should not be a chore. We don't have to talk about the heavy stuff every time, but at the same time we shouldn't spend all of our time discussing the basic running of our lives. "Have you called the plumber? Have you paid those bills? Who's taking the kids to soccer practice?" These are all things we need to discuss, but they don't help us connect on a deeper level.

We Have to Make The Time

In the first chapter on Time, I asked for 8 hours of time spent together per week. This usually breaks down to about one hour each day during the week and a date night on the weekend. Most couples ask me, "How the heck are we going to come up with 8 hours every week!?" Well, the first thing you can do is turn off your electronic equipment; TV's, computers, blackberries, etc. and specifically take them out of your bedroom today! Research shows that couples without a television in their bedroom have twice as much sex as couples that do have a TV in their bedroom and, if you're over 50, that statistic jumps to 5 times more sex!

For some couples, for many reasons, the one hour each weeknight is simply not possible. They must be more creative and come up with some other time to spend together. I know one couple that takes off work on Fridays once a month and they spend the whole day together from 8 am to 10 pm and have fun adventures around town.

We Must Prioritize Time Together

In any case, it is very rare that any of us will spontaneously stumble upon free time. Instead, we have to *make* the time. Investing in time alone together as a couple has to be your number one priority. I recommend that you sit down with your calendars on Sunday night and figure out the schedule for the week. The first thing you should tackle is: When are we going to schedule our 8 hours together this week? Scheduling this time together becomes a lot easier if you make it part of your regular routine. This will look different for every couple. An example: "How about, Monday and Thursday nights we agree that there's no TV or computer after the kids go to bed. We'll just grab a glass of wine, sit on our patio and talk. On Tuesday mornings, we meet for coffee before work. We always get together on Wednesdays for lunch and while we both agree we can't give up watching our favorite TV show on Thursday nights, we've arranged for a regular babysitter for four hours every Saturday night." There's your 8 hours! Not so hard, right? Wrong. Look, I understand; the reality is that life is complicated and throws us all curve balls and our lives get busy and nothing is this easy, but - I can't emphasize this enough — scheduling the time is critical.

 I saw a woman in my practice who had left her husband after 30 years of marriage. She had supported his career, she had raised their children, they had plenty of money, he was of an age to retire. During their entire marriage, she had asked him to spend time together. He never made it a priority. Then most recently, she had asked him to retire, so that they might travel and spend time together. He refused. She still loved him, but she left him after 30 years of marriage because he wouldn't commit to spending time together. Don't let this happen to you.

Spending Time Together
Makes Everything Easier

Everything is easier and more comfortable in your marriage once you spend more time alone together. In my experience, couples initially really struggle with this, but when they get it right, they come back week after week, more relaxed, more connected, and more in love with each other.

 **Exercise E: Calendar**

Now it's time to get out your calendars and schedule at least 8 hours a week together. On the next two pages you'll see an **example** of such a calendar as well as two **blank** calendars for your convenience. The example calendar highlights the "Alone Time." Those are the times that count toward your 8 hours. The blank calendar is for you to complete with your partner. Make sure you schedule at least 8 hours of alone time together.

(Example Family Calendar for the Week)

	Sun	Mon	Tues	Wed	Thur	Fri	Sat
6							
7		------Get Kids Ready / School Drop off------					
8	Clean Garage	Yoga	Coffee		Yoga		
9							Soccer
10							
11							Target
12	Family						Lunch
1	Fun			Lunch			Groceries
2	Day						BD Party
3	At	Math Tutoring			Dentist appt		
4	Beach!		Piano Lesson	Tennis Lesson			
5		Soccer Practice			Soccer Practice		
6	Family Dinner		Family Dinner	Family Dinner		BBQ At	Date
7	--------Backpacks, Baths, Bedtime----------					The Jones'	Night
8	Fill out calendar	Laundry Bills	B-ball w/ the	Grown Up TV	Straighten House		Jazz
9		No TV/ electronics	guys	Time	No TV/ electronics		Club
10							
11							

Shaded = Time Alone, Counts toward 8 hour goal

(Copy #1)

StrongMarriageNow Calendar
Week of:_____

	Sun	Mon	Tues	Wed	Thur	Fri	Sat
6							
7							
8							
9							
10							
11							
12							
1							
2							
3							
4							
5							
6							
7							
8							
9							
10							
11							

If you'd like to have a full page copy of the
calendar go to:
http://strongmarriagenow.com/calendar

(Copy #2)

StrongMarriageNow Calendar
Week of:_____

	Sun	Mon	Tues	Wed	Thur	Fri	Sat
6							
7							
8							
9							
10							
11							
12							
1							
2							
3							
4							
5							
6							
7							
8							
9							
10							
11							

If you'd like to have a full page copy of the calendar go to:
http://strongmarriagenow.com/calendar

What You Need To Know

1. Time Together Alone:

    a. Must be in a place where you can **make eye contact** with each other.

    b. Happens when you can **talk only with each other** for a significant, uninterrupted block of time.

    c. Occurs somewhere you can **both let your guard down.**

2. Making the time is easier when it becomes part of your regular routine.

3. You will never just find the time. **You must make the time.** Get your calendars out and commit to the time!

Chapter 4

Plan the Time

In this chapter, you will learn how to:

- Follow ground rules for your *Time Alone Together*
- Be clear about your objectives
- Choose a location
- Go on dates without breaking the bank

Now, I'd like to discuss some important ground rules for your Time Alone Together as well as talk about how to best choose and plan your together activities.

First, the ground rules for your time together. Following these rules will make your time together more meaningful and successful.

Make Your Time Together Special by Following These Ground Rules

1. **Be Present** – When you are together you need to have your mind in the moment; you need to pay attention to each other. Put away your phone and electronics. Of course you will answer your phone if there is an emergency, but the whole point of this is to have quality time with the person you love *without distractions*. Now is not the time to be waiting for that business call from New York, or to be figuring out that personnel problem at work, or even to be thinking about how you're going to get the stain out of your shirt. Put all of that away and pay attention to your spouse.

2. **Be flexible** – If you are at a park or the beach and it starts to rain, duck into a coffee shop. If the museum you were both looking forward to seeing is closed, go to a paint-your-own pottery place and see if either of you suddenly became artistic (maybe you both already are!). The point is, find something else to do. Be willing to explore and be spontaneous – just do it together.

3. **Take turns choosing what to do** – This does not mean, however, that you must take turns making it happen. In most relationships, one person usually has the role of planning and organizing the activities. I call this person the "Entertainment Director." The

truth is that person is typically better at it! If you're the "Entertainment Director" in your relationship, embrace your talent and be happy about it. Try not to be resentful. I often hear, "If he loved me, he would plan a date." This simply isn't true. Would you feel the same way about him cutting your hair? Let's say your husband is a doctor who knows nothing of hair styling. Would you say, "If he loved me, he would cut and highlight my hair?" Uh, I think once you came back with super-short, orange and purple hair, you might change your mind. So let's just give up on the idea that we want people to have talents they simply don't have. The fact is, we're all good at different things and usually one person is better at planning activities than the other. Just go with it and don't let this get in the way of you connecting as a couple. (And for crying out loud, don't end up with orange and purple hair!)

4. **Have a good attitude** – Get on board and have fun, especially if you are *not* the "Entertainment Director." Appreciate the thought and the work that went into planning the activity and help to make it special. Do <u>not</u> take the "Entertainment Director" for granted!!

5. **Be positive** – Your mood is your choice. Let me say that another way – no one is responsible for how you feel except you. You can choose to think about and dwell upon all the stressful things in your life (or the

situation) or you can choose to pay attention to your spouse and all the things for which you are truly grateful. This is often a tough concept for people to understand and accept, so here's an illustration. Have you ever been out to a really nice restaurant and the service that day is horrible, the food takes forever to get there and the person at the next table is being really loud? Well, you could choose to focus on all that and let it ruin your night OR you could choose to pay attention to your wonderful spouse, appreciate that you can afford to dine at such a nice establishment and be thankful for all the things that are going *right* in your life. Both perspectives are options. *You* decide what to pay attention to and therefore, *you* decide how you feel. So when you're spending time alone with your spouse, remember to take responsibility for your own mood, (it's not anyone else's job to "make" you feel happy – that's your job!) so <u>choose</u> to have a good time!

Successful Together Activities
Take Planning

Many of you are successful in life and/or in business and you know how to plan and execute an event. You know a successful event has a clear objective, the right location and a budget. Planning a date is just that simple.

1. **Clear Objective** – Our number one objective is to connect with each other. Sometimes you just want to go out and have a light, happy time together and

sometimes you have a tough topic that needs to be discussed. Both of these are very important. Keep in mind that laughing and having a good time is just as important to connecting as discussing your deepest, innermost thoughts and feelings. Try to find a balance and make time for both.

2. **Location** – That's simpler; as discussed, a good location is any place where you can let your guard down and have a conversation. That is why sitting next to each other in a movie theater doesn't count, but sitting on your own patio and talking does count. Exercising together counts if there's an opportunity to talk. (If you can run and talk at the same time – more power to you!) Believe it or not, going to Home Depot counts, as long as it's just the two of you and you feel comfortable having an in-depth conversation in Home Depot! A deck of cards on your kitchen table, getting takeout and going to the park, reading this book together at the beach – all of these locations offer an opportunity to talk to each other and therefore connect.

3. **Budget** – Interestingly, this is the number one excuse I most often hear in therapy, regardless of a couples' income. Most people simply have a hard time spending money on this. They'll spend $200 an hour on therapy, but they won't get a baby sitter for $40 and go watch the sunset together. And what many couples simply don't realize is that time alone doesn't have to cost *any* money at all. Below, we've

included a list of more than one hundred Together Activities.

Keep Your Marriage Fun and Exciting!

Let's face it. Monogamy can be boring. Marriages can end up in a rut with the same routines, activities, restaurants, etc. One of the components of falling in love in the first place is the newness of the experience, the thrilling exploration of undiscovered territory, the excitement of encountering a whole new world together. After just a few years of marriage, we don't run across many things that are new and/or surprising anymore. Therefore, we must create this for ourselves, designing new experiences, exploring new territory and expanding our world together.

We've put together a list of Together Activities to help keep your marriage fun and exciting for years to come. Try a few or come up with your own. But, whatever you do and however you do it, *please* try to consistently spend at least 8 hours a week of time alone together. It may well be the most important thing you do for your marriage.

If you haven't done so already, now would be a good time to take our Marriage Success Quiz and find out if your marriage has what it takes to make it: http://strongmarriagenow.com/successquiz

Together Activities

Here are more than 100 ideas of activities that you and your spouse can do together!

Free Activities
1. Make a puzzle
2. Go for a hike
3. Do Tai Chi or yoga
4. Stroll through a historic neighborhood
5. Stretch
6. Go for a walk in a new part of town
7. Explore downtown on foot
8. Go for a jog
9. Go for a bike ride
10. Work in the garden
11. Play cards
12. Hang out on the patio
13. Write and discuss a gratitude list
14. Listen to music
15. Go to a park
16. Go to the beach
17. Go to the lake or river
18. WIndow-shop
19. Checkout a museum on it's free day
20. Browse book stores
21. Choose books together at the library
22. Go for a scenic drive
23. Check out the open houses in your neighborhood
24. Sit on a park bench and people watch
25. Play a board game
26. Dance in your living room
27. Go to a concert in the park
28. Sit by the fire
29. Watch the sunset
30. Wander around on the boardwalk
31. Sunbathe together
32. Go to an art fair
33. Walk the dog
34. Play with your pets

35. Bathe or shower together
36. Give each other back massages
37. Foot rubbing
38. Help each other with chores
39. Show each other where you played as kids
40. Revisit places where you had fun earlier in your relationship - Reminisce and connect
41. Go stargazing
42. Make a home movie together
43. Splash around in the rain
44. Pop into an art gallery
45. Play Frisbee
46. Play soccer
47. Go roller skating
48. Fly a kite
49. Look up ""Hidden spots"" in your city on the web and go to one
50. Go swimming
51. Skinny-dip
52. Hang out in a Jacuzzi

Low-Cost ($) Activities
1. Workout at the gym
2. Go kayaking
3. Go out for coffee
4. Go on a picnic
5. Work on an art project
6. Visit a local holiday celebration
7. Find and make recipes together
8. Go berry picking
9. Go see a local band
10. Go camping
11. Go out for ice cream
12. Go bowling
13. Play a round of miniature golf
14. Go to "Annual events - car shows, boat shows, gardening shows"
15. Run errands
16. Go to a local mall

17. Take advantage of 2-for-1 coupons - checkout Restaurant.com for great deals
18. Go to the farmers market
19. Go ice skating
20. Checkout a nearby town (shops or restaurants?)

Affordable ($$) Activities
1. Watch **StrongMarriageNow** videos
2. Work on a home improvement project
3. Go out for lunch
4. Go wine tasting
5. Rent a paddleboat
6. Go sailing
7. See a sporting event
8. Go to a county fair
9. Go out dancing
10. Go to the zoo
11. Go to an arcade
12. Go out to dinner
13. Go whale watching
14. Play a round of golf
15. Shop for bedroom toys
16. Go to a Wine Bar or Lounge
17. Sing Karaoke
18. Go rock climbing
19. Go horseback riding
20. Go on a riverboat cruise
21. Go on harbor cruise
22. Go on a gondola ride
23. Go on a romantic train ride
24. Go out for a drink and appetizers

Splurge ($$$) Activities
1. Go to a concert
2. Go to an amusement park
3. Take dance lessons
4. Go on a dinner cruise
5. Go to dinner at a fancy restaurant
6. Get tickets to a concert you really want to see

7. Have a "Staycation" - Spend a night at a hotel in your own city
8. Ride Segways (upright scooters)
9. Go boating
10. Go to dinner and a comedy show
11. Go on a horse and buggy ride

Extravagant ($$$$) Activities
1. Go scuba diving
2. Go on hot air balloon ride
3. Go skiing / snowboarding
4. Weekend Getaways

Exercise F: Together Activities

The whole point of together activities is to spend <u>Time Alone Together</u>. Remember that your number one objective is to connect with each other. This can happen in any location where you can let your guard down and talk with each other.

I recommend that each of you take a look at the previous list of more than 100 ideas and choose 10 things you'd like to do together, (feel free to come up with your own ideas!). Then sit down and discuss the objective, the location and the budget. And remember, have FUN!

What You Need To Know

1. **Follow the ground rules** for alone time to build your relationship:
    a. Be present
    b. Be flexible
    c. Take turns choosing what to do.
    d. Have a good attitude.
    e. Be positive.

2. **Planning your activities ensures success**
    a. Have a clear objective. Remember that the primary objective is to connect with each other. Keep in mind that laughing and having a good time is just as connecting as discussing your deep, innermost thoughts and feelings.
    b. Choose the right location. This is any place where you can let your guard down and have a conversation.
    c. Agree on the budget. Don't let this get in the way. Alone time doesn't have to cost any money.

3. **Keep your marriage fun and exciting!**

What You Can Do To Spend Time Together

Here are the **Marriage Success System** *To-Do's* for this section:

1. Make your marriage your **number one priority.**

2. **Schedule 8 hours** a week of alone together time.

3. **Choose** your top 10 Together Activities and plan at least one and make it fun!

4. Continue to **Tell, Text or Email** your partner every day at least one thing that you appreciate about him/her.

5. Note another one of your partner's top marriage priorities (review Exercise B: What Kind of Marriage Do You Want to Build that was part of Section I in the **Marriage Success System**) and go out of your way to **meet that need** some time this week.

Be sure to go to Appendix B, cut out your Commitment Cards and post them where each of you will see them every day.

Section III:
Understanding Each Other

In this section you're going to learn:

- How to forgive so you can move forward
- How to effectively apologize
- How to let go of the past and have a new beginning
- How humor makes everything easier
- The importance of giving your partner the *"Benefit of the Doubt"*
- How to honor each other's feelings and deepen your connection
- Why couples get stuck on long-standing issues

Chapter 5

Forgiveness, Effectively Apologizing and a New Beginning

In this chapter, you will learn:

- The importance of forgiveness
- The 7 steps to an effective apology
- The impact of past pain
- An essential Marriage Golden Rule
- How to let go and move forward

To begin the section on **Understanding Each Other**, we must first understand and acknowledge that many of you feel hurt and angry, scared and/or confused and have felt that way for a long time. It is vital, however, to recognize that *your partner feels the same way*. Though you may feel like you are the wronged party, I can all but guarantee that they feel the same. Consequently, before we can even begin to work on the relationship, we must first forgive our partners and ourselves for the state of the relationship today.

As you might imagine, being able to forgive someone is one of the most essential skills in a long-term happy marriage because, let's face it, we're all human, we all married someone human, and all humans make mistakes. Some of these mistakes are minor and some can be life-altering. But in order to move forward and feel safe and happy in a marriage, all of these mistakes must be forgiven.

Here, I'm going to define forgiveness, explain the importance of forgiveness to both the marriage and to the individual, and discuss seven common issues that may be getting in the way of offering forgiveness.

Defining Forgiveness

Forgiveness is often defined as letting go of resentment, indignation or anger as a result of a *perceived* offense, difference of opinion or mistake. In other words, it's about letting go of the feelings that were hurt when we thought the other person "messed up." I also believe that forgiveness entails no longer seeking or demanding punishment or restitution for that perceived offense. In other words, forgiveness has two parts - letting go and moving forward.

Why does forgiveness matter? Well, there are lots of great comments about this. Bernard Meltzer said:

> *"When you forgive, you in no way change the past - but you sure do change the future."*

Said another way, the past can't be changed. It has already happened and there's nothing either of us can do about it. What we're left with, then, is a choice about how we intend to go on. Yes, I said a choice. Forgiveness is in our control. It's ours to give or withhold and we can choose whether we want to be stuck living in the past, holding onto our pain, or living for today and the future, and letting go. We can only let go if we forgive. Lewis Smedes said:

> *"To forgive is to set a prisoner free and discover that the prisoner was you."*

When we refuse to forgive, we keep the past alive in our thoughts. These thoughts can be so vivid that we feel as if the pain is re-occurring again and again in the present moment. But in the end, who does that really hurt? By repeatedly focusing on the pain from a past experience, you continue to relive it and often times expand upon it. Not only do you allow the pain from the past to continue to damage the relationship, you choose to let it repeatedly damage you. To illustrate that, Maya Angelou said:

> *"Resentment is like drinking poison and expecting the other person to die."*

To withhold forgiveness damages not only the relationship, but also yourself and, therefore, your future.

Why Do We Have a
Hard Time Forgiving?

Now that you know the importance of forgiveness, let's cover the seven common reasons that make it hard to forgive.

Reason 1: We Don't Understand Why They Did What They Did

The first reason we have a hard time forgiving is because we don't understand or we misunderstand what's really going on with our partner. In other words, we don't understand *why they did what they did.*

The most common explanation for their behavior is what I like to call **"An Emotional Broken Arm"** and I often explain it like this: When one walks around in the world in the perfect state of health, nothing hurts - everything is fine. When someone brushes up against them or accidentally steps on their toes, they respond with a somewhat calm, proportionate response like "Hey, careful, you brushed up against me." or "Ouch, you stepped on my toe. Please try not to do that again."

However, when one has a broken arm and someone brushes up against them, they feel unbearable pain and often times explode with "Aargh! How could you? I can't believe you did that!" or even worse, they attack back with something like, "You did that on purpose! What the heck is wrong with you? Get away from me!"

Emotional broken arms exist for many different reasons, including, but not limited to: the environment in which one grew up, past pain within the relationship itself or fear of the future; in particular, fear of being abandoned. But emotional broken arms may also stem from something as simple as a horrible day at work, bad news from loved ones, or sheer exhaustion.

In any case, when "brushed up against," these emotional broken arms lead people to say and do things out of pain that significantly injure their partner's feelings, doing damage to the relationship.

Many people are walking around in their marriages with the equivalent of emotional broken arms causing extreme reactions. And these reactions can really hurt their partner.

REAL LIFE EXAMPLES

Carl forgot to pick up the dry-cleaning again. When he arrived home, his (exhausted) wife, Anita, responded angrily with, "I'm tired of being the only one that does anything around here. I don't know if I can keep doing this!" Confused and hurt, Carl stormed off.

Or, Luke had a horrible day at work. Becky appeared to ignore Luke when he walked in the door because she was on the phone. He responded bitterly with, "You're so cold. All of our other friends' wives treat their husbands better than this!" Confused and hurt, Becky withdrew. For all intents and purposes, the first "mistakes" that Carl and Becky made (forgetting the dry cleaning and not hanging up the phone) can be considered minor "brushes." However, the results of these brushes caused excruciating emotional pain for Anita and Luke due to their respective emotional broken arms and their responses were both extreme and explosive.

On a side note, these types of instances usually start a *cycle* of emotional broken arms, i.e Carl stormed off after Anita yelled at him. Now she's hurt and confused about his reaction and, unless they work things out, now she has her own kind of emotional broken arm. Couples can be involved in and struggling with these cycles for years.

The cycle can only be broken in two ways: understanding your partner's "emotional broken arm" and/or understanding and controlling your own. If you understand that your reactions are being triggered by your own hurt feelings, you can choose to control those feelings and, therefore, handle the situation in a way that doesn't damage the relationship.

Understanding what's going on with your partner can simply be done by pausing, figuring out what's broken, finding compassion, and offering forgiveness. Understanding what's going on with you can be accomplished by going through the same steps - pause, ask yourself what's really going on, be honest and offer compassion. Taking the time to do either of these steps can end this destructive cycle.

In order to accomplish this understanding of each other, however, a couple must be able to communicate effectively. We discuss this further in upcoming chapters. For now, know that having an understanding of and compassion for what drove either of you to hurt the other can go a long way toward helping you forgive.

Reason 2: Believing that Forgiveness Condones the Behavior

The second reason many people find it difficult to forgive is that they believe offering forgiveness *condones* a behavior. They think that forgiving their partner will communicate to their partner that whatever they did was okay. Interestingly enough, that's even sometimes how people attempt to offer forgiveness by off-handedly saying the words "That's okay," - when it's really not.

For forgiveness to flow freely, it's important that both people in the relationship understand that forgiving someone does *not* mean you're telling them that what they did was okay, and it certainly does *not* mean you're giving them permission to do it again. It simply means that you understand that there may have been painful circumstances, misunderstandings or even accidents that contributed to the person's actions and you're choosing to pardon the behavior *this time*.

Reason 3: Holding Our Partner To A Higher Standard Than We Hold Ourselves

The third reason we find it difficult to forgive is that we tend to hold our partner to a different (usually higher) standard than we hold ourselves. The best way for me to illustrate this is for me to tell you a personal story.

I don't know if you know this, but when one goes to graduate school to become a psychologist, one has to participate in therapy - *a lot of therapy*. So, at the beginning of graduate school, I participated in individual therapy and found it quite helpful. But after a time, I found that I'd worked through most of my personal issues.

Shortly thereafter, I got married and decided it would be fun to experience couples therapy. Now, I'm sure it does not surprise you to learn that new psychology graduate students think they know an awful lot about an awful lot. So, in one particular couples therapy session, I was righteously explaining to the therapist all of the things my husband did "wrong" in the marriage (picture me ticking off reason after reason on my fingers). It was at that point that I received probably some of the best marriage advice I have ever heard. She turned to me and said, "Who the heck do you think you are?" (And let me tell you, she didn't actually use the word heck). I was livid! She went on to say, "Sweetheart, the next time you start making a list of everything he does wrong, take a good hard look at yourself." Well, let me tell you, I was still livid! However, I went home that night and started to think and, of course, realized that, well, maybe, on occasion, I am no peach to live with either! I have many faults (none of which I'm going to tell you about now.) Suffice it to say, to this day, when my husband does something that hurts my feelings, makes me angry or simply perplexes me, I say to myself "Dana, who the heck do you think you are?" and I choose to forgive him.

So, I hope you can see this as the gift I *eventually* did. Next time your partner does something to hurt your feelings, make you angry or simply confuse you, ask yourself if you're holding them to a higher standard than you hold yourself and then ask yourself, "Who do you think you are?"

Reason 4: Scorekeeping

The fourth reason people find it difficult to forgive is what I like to call the "You hurt me worse" or "You hurt me first" game. Have you ever been in a fight and one of you has said "You did blank, blank and blank to me" and the other one of you responded with, "Yeah, but I only did that because you did blank, blank and blank to me first!"

A real life example of this is "You promised you'd call me when you were going to be late coming home from work, and you didn't!" "Yeah, but you promised *me* you would stop leaving your clothes all over the floor and the bedroom was a mess today!" This scorekeeping game results in a reluctance to apologize *and* a reluctance to forgive. In other words, I'm not going to apologize because you hurt me first, and/or I'm not going to forgive you because you hurt me worse. Unfortunately, in this game, **nobody** wins. We just go on hurting each other, often for years and years. To break this pattern, try and see each instance, each mistake, intentional or otherwise, as it's own singular event. Attempt to understand it, as I explained before, offer forgiveness and move forward.

Reason 5: Expecting a Guarantee

The fifth reason people struggle with forgiveness is because they're waiting for a guarantee that the behavior will never happen again before they're willing to forgive. Unfortunately, as none of us are fortune-tellers, we cannot predict the future and therefore, cannot offer this guarantee. Lily Tomlin said simply:

"Forgiveness means giving up all hope of a better past."

Notice that the decision to forgive is not contingent on an apology, or even a promise to never do it again. It is simply a decision to let go of the past and focus on the future. It is not, in fact, a guarantee of a *better* future. As I keep saying, forgiveness is simply a willingness to let go of the past and move forward.

However, I will grant that it is extremely difficult, if not impossible to forgive if the transgression continues to happen. The most obvious example of this is an affair. We cannot forgive and move forward if it's still happening. Clearly some behavior has to stop. This concept might even be difficult to apply to small transgressions. It's really hard to forgive you for leaving your clothes on the floor if it's been happening every day for the last 10 years!

I would like to mention, however, that for smaller transgressions, there is an alternative. It's rather controversial, but let me tell you, it can lead to a happier marriage and a happier life. Are you ready? You could simply *choose* to happily pick up the clothes yourself and decide to forgive your partner for their life-long inability to locate the laundry hamper. This one's a lot easier to do if you ask yourself that "Who the heck do you think you are?" question first.

Reason 6: An Unwilingness to Give Up Power

The sixth reason that people find it difficult to forgive is a belief that to offer forgiveness is to relinquish power. And, they're not completely wrong. If you are seeking forgiveness from me and I am withholding it, I am in the position of power. That is, in fact, true. But only for as long as the person seeks forgiveness. As soon as they stop, that power is gone. So, I must ask myself, what is that power gaining me and what is maintaining that power costing me? It gains me a temporary feeling of righteousness, superiority and control. But it costs so much more. It costs me intimacy, trust and connection. Be careful about withholding forgiveness to maintain power. In the end, you're really the one who will pay for it.

If you feel that offering forgiveness makes you weak, gullible or naive, let me tell you what Ghandi said:

"The weak can never forgive. Forgiveness is an attribute of the strong."

I know it can be scary and difficult, but I encourage you to be brave, find your strength and choose to forgive.

Reason 7: Ineffective Apologies

Now it's time to discuss the seventh common reason why people find it difficult to forgive. Most people don't know how to offer an effective apology

So many couples find themselves endlessly fighting over the same issues over and over - constantly bringing up transgressions and hurt feelings from the past. One of the main reasons this happens has to do with a lack of listening to each other and never feeling truly heard which we will discuss at greater length in the next chapter.

But the other reason people find themselves hanging on to resentment and bringing up past issues is that forgiveness was never truly offered. Once trust has been broken in a relationship, it can be extremely difficult to mend, ironically, even if both parties are willing to fix it. While I discussed a number of the common issues that get in the way of forgiveness above, I saved this one for last because it's extremely important and can be one of the hardest skills to master. It is quite simply the art of an effective apology.

Many of us are "taught" how to apologize from the time we can speak. Our parents tell us, "You took your brother's toy, say 'you're sorry.'" Or, "You hurt your friend's feelings, say you're sorry," or even, "You stole that gum from the market, tell the manager you're sorry." While it's extremely important that we were taught to say these words, in all of these cases, the genuineness of the apology is questionable – we likely don't really mean it. Oh, we're sorry all right. We're sorry we got caught. We're sorry we're grounded. And we're particularly sorry we have to apologize. But that's not really what "sorry" is supposed to mean.

Now, fast-forward to your average married couple.

> *"You spent too much money again,"*
> *"Sorry, but I really needed that (fill in the blank)"*

> *"You hurt my feelings when you spoke to me that way,"*
> *"Sorry, you're feelings got hurt."*

and even,

> *"I'm absolutely devastated you cheated on me."*
> *"I'm sorry, but I've been telling you for years that I haven't been happy and you haven't been listening to me!"*

Some of these examples may be truly heart-felt apologies but because they are incomplete they rarely lead to forgiveness.

A true and effective apology has seven important parts. I know this sounds like a lot, but don't worry; it becomes almost second nature once you truly understand these parts. *All* the parts are important because effectively apologizing makes it easier for the injured party to believe you are genuinely remorseful, accept your apology and forgive you. An effective apology shows you are serious about making amends and repairing the relationship, To help you with this, we've included an exercise after this chapter called "Prepare to Apologize."

The Seven Steps of an Effective Apology

Step 1: Determine What Actually Happened

In order to truly apologize, you need to know what you're apologizing for. What happened? What was *your* part in it? And how did it make your partner feel? Unless all of these questions are answered, the apology is likely to be ineffective as you may be apologizing for only part of what occurred or for the completely wrong thing.

When I say it's important to understand what happened, what I mean is, it's important to understand your partner's *perception* of what happened. So many apologies are stalled at this stage because it begins a debate over "the facts." "You did this." "No I didn't, I did this." "Well, you said that." "Well, maybe, but I meant that." When you are attempting to offer a sincere apology, *your* perception of the facts is irrelevant. In order to apologize you must understand <u>what your partner believes happened</u>.

Next, you must determine what was your part in the situation. This is a tough one, but to sincerely apologize you must understand how your behavior contributed to the problem. Again, don't get caught up in who's right, who's wrong and who started it. Simply attempt to understand what your partner believes you did or didn't do.

It's important to note, however, that this is required regardless of whether your part in the situation was intentional or unintentional, meaning many people believe that they do not need to apologize for something they did accidentally or without malicious intent. If you didn't mean to step on your partner's foot but they're jumping around saying "Ow, Ow, Ow!" you would, of course, apologize. So, even if you did not intend to hurt your partner's feelings, if they are hurt, an apology is in order.

Now, I say your partner's feelings, because a sincere apology requires an understanding of how the situation *made your partner feel.* Often times, we assume we know how our partner feels when, in fact, we really don't. This usually occurs because we tend to see the world through our own eyes so we assume the effects of the incident are similar to what they would be if it happened to us. In other words, "I don't see the big deal if I forget to call you when I say I will. It wouldn't bother me, so I assume that it doesn't bother you all that much either." (See, even if you tell me it bothers you, I still have a hard time getting it, because it would *not bother me.*) But let's face it. Everybody's different, so we have to take the time to figure out how our *partner* felt about the incident. Not doing so could lead to an ineffective and, therefore, unaccepted apology, because the apology never addressed the real feelings involved. All three of the parts – What happened? What was *your* part in it? And how did it make your partner feel? – require some thoughtful questioning and some careful listening.

Here's an example of what that might sound like. "Hey honey, you seem upset. Can you tell me what's up? How are you feeling?" Now remember, it's important to simply listen to their point of view and seek to truly understand what your partner believes happened.

After you asked how your partner was feeling, let's suppose you found out they were hurt because they felt you were in a bad mood during dinner and snapped at them multiple times. An example of an apology for this would be,

| APOLOGY EXAMPLE | "I'm sorry I hurt your feelings when I snapped at you during dinner. |

Step 2: Figure Out Why It Happened

Determining why something happened is an extremely important component because unless the apologizer knows why an incident happened, they cannot make every effort to keep it from happening again. And unless they are able to express why it happened to their partner, it will be extremely difficult for their partner to offer forgiveness because their partner is likely scared that they will be hurt again. However, as I previously mentioned, because none of us can predict the future, none of us can guarantee we will never hurt our partner again. Nevertheless, understanding why something hurtful occurred increases the probability that we will be able to prevent that incident from happening again.

Keep in mind, there is a difference between an explanation and an excuse. It is sometimes difficult for the injured party to hear the explanation of why something occurred because they interpret it as an excuse. Both parties, therefore, need to keep in mind that an explanation of the behavior does not excuse the behavior, it simply sheds further light on the event.

So, you've asked how your partner was feeling, and found out they were hurt because they believed you were in a bad mood during dinner and snapped at them several times. An example of an apology with an explanation for this would be,

APOLOGY EXAMPLE	"I'm sorry I hurt your feelings when I snapped at you during dinner. I'm really stressed about work and have a lot on my mind."

An example of an excuse is, "I'm sorry I snapped at you during dinner, BUT I'm really stressed about work and have a lot on my mind." It's a small word, but the word "but" negates everything you said before, including the "I'm sorry" part, and changes that explanation into an excuse.

Step 3: *Sincerely* Express Regret

I say "sincerely" because some people voice their apology, or more accurately use a *tone* of voice in their apology, that seems *insincere*, "Sorry, already," or *guarded*, "Fine. Sorry," or even *hostile*, "What, I said I was sorry!" As you can imagine, none of these tones are effective because people can tell when you are or *are not* sincerely asking for forgiveness. Therefore, be sure to use your most kind, loving, and respectful tone of voice when you say,

APOLOGY EXAMPLE

"I'm sorry I hurt your feelings when I snapped at you during dinner. I'm really stressed about work and have a lot on my mind."

Step 4: Accept Responsibility

Accepting Responsibility is another essential component to an effective apology. Saying something like "I am sorry that *you* got your feelings hurt during dinner," puts the responsibility on the injured party. Additionally, "I'm sorry that *you* feel that way," or "I am sorry that *you* reacted that way," or worse "I am sorry, but *you* shouldn't have made me do it in the first place," do *not* take responsibility. These types of statements convey a message that you are sorry that *the other person* is in the wrong for misinterpreting *you*, is *too* sensitive, or is, in fact, to blame. Not surprisingly, this lack of responsibility doesn't help them forgive you.

"I am sorry" should always include, "I am sorry that *I* did or didn't do something" and it only works if you really mean it! In this case a sincere apology sounds something like:

"I'm sorry I hurt your feelings when I snapped at you during dinner. I'm really stressed about work and have a lot on my mind. But I am really sorry that I hurt your feelings."

Step 5: Make Every Effort *Not* To Do It Again

When apologizing, it's important to make every effort not to repeat the offense. You may be asking, why I didn't say *promise* not to repeat the offense. I've got to tell you that I'm not really fond of "promises." I don't think one should regularly make promises in a marriage other than to be faithful, to work on the relationship and to stay married. I don't think one should regularly make "promises" because they are too easily broken. The truth is, we're all human and life happens.

Here's an illustration of why I think "promises" in this scenario are a bad idea. "I'm sorry I hurt your feelings when I snapped at you during dinner. I promise I'll never do it again." Really? Can you truly keep that promise? As human beings, we're not perfect and we all make mistakes. The truth is, you really *can't* promise that you'll never be in a bad mood and snippy again. If you do "promise" this, as your partner, I simply won't believe you, and therefore, can't forgive you. Now, here's the alternative –

APOLOGY EXAMPLE

"I'm sorry I hurt your feelings when I snapped at you during dinner. I'm really stressed about work and have a lot on my mind. But I'm really sorry that I hurt your feelings. I'm going to try to make dinnertime about us and leave my stress about work at the office."

In other words, you're going to give it your best shot. That, your partner can believe, and therefore, more readily forgive.

The point here is to make *every effort* not to do it again. This then, takes a plan. Many times, our intentions are pure. We don't want to hurt our partner and we really believe we're never going to do it again. The part that many people forget however, is – how are they going to ensure they never do it again. What's the plan? Or more accurately, what's the alternative course of action to what already occurred? Continuing with our current apology,

APOLOGY EXAMPLE

"I'm sorry I hurt your feelings when I snapped at you during dinner. I'm really stressed about work and have a lot on my mind. But I'm really sorry that I hurt your feelings. I'm going to try to make dinnertime about us and leave my stress about work at the office. I think I'll put my phone in another room during dinner so I don't keep getting pulled back into work stuff."

Now there's a plan. Terrific! But let me give you a really important tip: don't bluff. Having a plan so you don't mess up in the future is important, but if you're bluffing or you're not able to (or don't intend to) stick to the plan, not only will the plan not work, it may actually make things worse (remember "promises?"). Understand that if the same transgression occurs over and over, it makes it far more difficult for the injured party to forgive, because it's far more difficult for them to believe things will ever change. Do not make the mistake of believing that simply because the injured party forgave you the last two times they will forgive you a third time.

So before you offer to leave your phone in another room during dinner, make darn sure you can stick to your word and leave it there or come up with another plan.

Step 6: Make Amends

The sixth step of an effective apology is to figure out what you can do to make things right. Okay, let's face it, forgiving somebody for being snippy at dinner is pretty easy to do, but sometimes the transgressions are much bigger. In these cases, it helps to offer restitution, to offer to do or say something that will help mend the damage.

If you ruined dinner by snapping at your partner, offer to make reservations for a special dinner the next night. If you said something really mean, write a note telling your partner everything you love about them. And for the much larger issues – if you engaged in an inappropriate relationship, make sure you do *everything* your partner needs to re-establish trust regardless of the inconvenience to you. Many times, we say we simply don't know what will make it easier for our partner to forgive us. In that case, the best way to find out is to ask, "What can I do to make things right?" Sometimes your partner won't automatically know, so be patient. But when they tell you what you can do to make amends, go ahead and do it.

APOLOGY EXAMPLE

"I'm sorry I hurt your feelings when I snapped at you during dinner. I'm really stressed about work and have a lot on my mind. But I'm really sorry that I hurt your feelings. I'm going to try to make dinner-time about us and leave my stress about work at the office. I think I'll put my phone in another room during dinner so I don't keep getting pulled back into work stuff. Can I make it up to you? How about I make dinner reservations for tomorrow night and we'll go out?"

Step 7: Request Forgiveness

I would argue that asking for forgiveness is, in fact, the hardest step and takes a considerable amount of courage, because, as I previously mentioned, honestly asking for forgiveness puts one in an incredibly vulnerable position. And while it is possible for one to forgive their partner without a request for forgiveness, allowing oneself to be humble and actually asking for it makes it a heck of a lot easier for our partner to forgive.

Interestingly, many people in a marriage make the mistake of believing that forgiveness is *owed* to them. And while I certainly advocate for free flowing forgiveness in a marriage, do not kid yourself into thinking you deserve it simply by being married. Forgiveness is always a gift. It should not be demanded; it should not be expected or assumed; it should *only* be humbly and patiently requested.

This "patient" part brings me to an important side note: understand that determining when it's time to accept an apology is <u>up to the injured party</u>. *When* they choose to hear your apology and *when* they choose to offer forgiveness is up to them. Pushing the issue and the timing so that *you* can hurry up and feel better does not help your cause. Instead, allow your partner the time and space for their feelings to cool down. When you don't allow for this space and time, your partner is likely to stall the forgiveness process. Therefore, be patient and allow *them* to determine when to forgive you. Doing this will actually move the forgiveness process along. So, once again, back to our current apology,

"I'm sorry I hurt your feelings when I snapped at you during dinner. I'm really stressed about work and have a lot on my mind. But I'm really sorry that I hurt your feelings. I'm going to try to make dinnertime about us and leave my stress about work at the office. I think I'll put my phone in another room during dinner so I don't keep getting pulled back into work stuff. Can I make it up to you? How about I make dinner reservations for tomorrow night and we'll go out? Anyway, I am sorry, will you please forgive me?"

Then allow them the time and space to process their feelings and accept your apology.

So to wrap up, let's recap the seven steps to an effective apology.

1. Determine *what* actually happened
2. Figure out *why* it happened
3. Sincerely express regret
4. Accept responsibility
5. Make every effort to not do it again
6. Make amends
7. Request forgiveness

It is only after we truly ask for and offer forgiveness that we can move forward and have the lifetime of trust, love, and happiness that we truly desire.

Exercise G1: Apologizing Effectively

Step 1a: Determine what actually happened. Ask yourself and your partner the following questions: What happened? What was *my* part in it? How did it make your partner feel?

> *"Hey honey, you seem upset. Can you tell me what's up? How are you feeling?"*

Step 1b: Make the apology

1. "I'm sorry I hurt your feelings when I_____

_____

_____

Step 2: Figure Out Why It Happened

2. "I said (or did) this because_____

_____

_____

Step 3: *Sincerely* express regret (Remember tone of voice!)

3. Practice using a kind, loving, respectful tone of voice in the apology you wrote above.

Step 4. Accept responsibility

4. "But I'm still sorry that what I said or did hurt your feelings."_____

_____

Step 5. Make every effort not to do it again
(Remember, have a workable plan!)

5. "I'm going to try to _____

_____

_____

I think I'll/we'll _____

_____

_____

Step 6. Make amends (Figure out what you can say or do to make things right.)

6. "Can I make it up to you?" Or "How can I make it up to you?"_____

_____

_____

Step 7. Request forgiveness (Remember, allow them the time and space to process their feelings and accept your apology.)

7. "I am sorry. Will you please forgive me?"_____

_____

_____

Putting It All Together:

1. "I'm sorry I hurt your feelings when I_____
_____
_____

2. "I said (or did) this because_____
_____
_____
_____

3. Practice using a kind, loving, respectful tone of voice in the apology you wrote above.

4. "But I'm still sorry that what I said or did hurt your feelings."_____

_____

5. "I'm going to try to _____
_____
_____

I think I'll/we'll _____
_____
_____

6. "Can I make it up to you?" Or "How can I make it up to you?"_____
_____
_____

7. "I am sorry. Will you please forgive me?"_____
_____
_____

Exercise G2: Apologizing Effectively

Step 1a: Determine what actually happened. Ask yourself and your partner the following questions: What happened? What was *my* part in it? How did it make your partner feel?

> *"Hey honey, you seem upset. Can you tell me what's up? How are you feeling?"*

Step 1b: Make the apology

1. "I'm sorry I hurt your feelings when I_____
_____
_____

Step 2: Figure Out Why It Happened

2. "I said (or did) this because_____
_____
_____

Step 3: *Sincerely* express regret   (Remember tone of voice!)

3. Practice using a kind, loving, respectful tone of voice in the apology you wrote above.

Step 4. Accept responsibility

4. "But I'm still sorry that what I said or did hurt your feelings."_____

_____

Step 5. Make every effort not to do it again
(Remember, have a workable plan!)

5. "I'm going to try to _____

_____

_____

I think I'll/we'll _____

_____

_____

Step 6. Make amends (Figure out what you can say or do to make things right.)

6. "Can I make it up to you?" Or "How can I make it up to you?"_____

_____

_____

Step 7. Request forgiveness (Remember, allow them the time and space to process their feelings and accept your apology.)

7. "I am sorry. Will you please forgive me?"_____

_____

_____

Putting It All Together:

1. "I'm sorry I hurt your feelings when I_____

_____

_____

2. "I said (or did) this because_____

_____

_____

_____

3. Practice using a kind, loving, respectful tone of voice in the apology you wrote above.

4. "But I'm still sorry that what I said or did hurt your feelings."_____

_____

5. "I'm going to try to _____

_____

_____

I think I'll/we'll _____

_____

_____

6. "Can I make it up to you?" Or "How can I make it up to you?"_____

_____

_____

7. "I am sorry. Will you please forgive me?"_____

_____

_____

Here are some examples of sincere apologies with an explanation, that accept responsibility, include a plan for ensuring the transgression does not happen again, make amends and ask for forgiveness:

> *"I'm truly sorry I hurt your feelings when I ignored you when you got home. I was finishing a phone call and didn't hear you come in. I'm really sorry that what I did hurt your feelings. I'm going to try to be more conscious of what time you get home. How about next time you get home, you tap me on the shoulder so that I know you're there and I can give you the hug that I want to? How can I make it up to you? Can I give you a big hug right now? Anyway, I am sorry, will you please forgive me?"*

> *"I'm genuinely sorry I hurt your feelings when I yelled at you when I got home. I had a horrible day at work today. I'm really sorry that what I said and how I said it hurt your feelings. I think next time I have such an awful day at work, I will just let you know and then take a little time by myself to cool down. Can I make it up to you? I wrote a note telling you everything I love about you. Anyway, I am sorry, will you please forgive me?"*

> *"I am so sorry that cheated on you. I have been unhappy in our marriage for a very long time. I'm really sorry that I betrayed your trust and hurt you so badly. I really care about you and our family and I want to work on the marriage with you. Let's set aside some time each week for each other and follow the steps in this book. I want to make this right. I will do whatever you need to earn your trust again. I am sorry. Will you please forgive me?"*

The Golden Rule

Finally, I want to end this section with one of the most important Golden Rules of Marriage:

> You must give in your marriage
> what you want to receive.

If you want to be trusted, you must trust. If you want kindness, you must be kind. If you want to be forgiven, you must forgive. And most importantly, if you want to be loved, you must give love. In the immortal words of one of the greatest bands of all time, The Beatles:

> "And in the end, the love you take
> is equal to the love you make."

In the following chapters, you'll learn how to understand your partner's perspective as well as to express your own feelings so that you can truly forgive, begin to heal, and move forward. This process is essential in the first step toward giving your marriage a new beginning.

New Beginning

So many people are frustrated in their marriage because they believe they have tried many different ways to improve the situation and these approaches didn't work. This is very common. There's a reason for this, however. Many people's efforts to fix their marriages in the past have failed because they used an ineffective approach based on incorrect information – they simply didn't know how. As I mentioned in the Foreword, if you wanted to learn how to swim, you wouldn't just keep hoping and drowning, you'd take swimming lessons!

Forgiveness, including learning how to apologize effectively and then beginning anew, depends on the recognition that you and your partner previously didn't have all the tools or skills needed to be successful in your marriage.

> Being happily married has very
> little to do with who you're married to.
> It has a lot more to do with
> knowing how to be happily married.

Therefore we suggest starting off with a clean slate. Apologize to one another, forgive each other and let go of the pain and frustration of the marriage you had prior to the **Marriage Success System**. Focus instead on learning these practical skills, applying them immediately and beginning your brand new, totally fulfilling marriage today.

Exercise H: A New Beginning

This is a ritual that some of you may want to perform to symbolize a fresh start to your marriage. This is particularly useful if you have painful situations that are interfering with your ability to move forward in your relationship. The purpose of the exercise is to forgive each other, let go of the marriage that you had before you learned the **Marriage Success System,** and to begin a new, happy, healthy relationship today.

Step 1: Complete information below symbolizing your marriage pre-Marriage Success System:
Get a piece of paper and write down the following:
* Wife's Name
* Husband's Name
* Date You Were Married
* Today's Date
* Any major painful memories that you want to let go

Step 2: Let the past go
Together, find a safe place to destroy (possibly even burn!) the paper symbolizing the state of your marriage up until now.

Step 3: Introduce Yourselves to Each Other
Turn to your partner, offer your hand and say "Hello, my name is _____.   Would you like to be happily married?"

Step 4:   Continue to apply the Marriage Success System.
Learn the information, apply the skills and remember to be positive, kind, and loving to each other.

What You Need To Know

- Forgiveness is essential if you want to have a happy healthy marriage.

- Understand and Avoid the 7 Reasons Why People Have a Difficult Time Forgiving:

    1. We don't understand why they did what they did

    2. Believing that forgiveness condones a behavior

    3. Holding our partner to a higher standard than we hold ourselves

    4. Scorekeeping

    5. Expecting a guarantee

    6. An unwillingness to give up power

    7. Ineffective apologies

- Practice the 7 Steps to An Effective Apology:

    1. Determine what actually happened

    2. Figure out why it happened

    3. Sincerely express regret

    4. Accept responsibility

    5. Make every effort not to do it again

    6. Make amends

    7. Request forgiveness

- We can and should forgive, let go of past hurt and move forward.

Chapter 6

Patience and Humor

In this chapter, you will learn:

- The positive impact of humor
- How to make everything easier
- The importance of giving your partner the *"Benefit of the Doubt"*
- What to do when your partner blows it

Be Patient with Yourself and Your Partner

When doing research to create this book, communication was the number one topic of interest and the number one area that couples wanted to improve in their marriages. Before diving into the mechanics of communication skills, however, I've found that a couple must first learn to consistently utilize patience and humor in their relationship. This can make communication considerably easier. Again, let me remind readers that these concepts take time to master. Consequently, be patient with yourselves and more importantly, be patient with each other as we go through this process.

Laughing at Ourselves and Our Situations Lightens Things Up

One of the easiest ways to access one's patience is to keep in touch with one's sense of humor. Much of the communication in a marriage can and should be fun and funny. We have got to be able to laugh at ourselves, and the situations we sometimes find ourselves in, or go quietly nuts. One of my favorite quotes reads, "Blessed are they who can laugh at themselves, for they shall never cease to be amused." The truth is monogamy can be hard and sometimes even annoying. If you don't have a sense of humor in a relationship, it's far more difficult to forgive and far more likely you'll feel like killing each other, (if you watch the news, people frequently do.) But if you can laugh together, it makes everything *sane*, it makes everything better and problems easier to solve. So, I challenge each of you to get back in touch with your sense of humor and look for the ridiculous, (trust me, it's there). It diffuses tension, makes you more receptive and helps you feel connected.

Having said this, let me be clear, when I'm talking about humor, I *never* mean humor at another person's expense. Be careful and aware of your partner's sensitivities. Some people hate to be teased, others are confused and hurt by sarcasm, while still others find these forms of communication hilarious and light-hearted. Know your partner and respect his/her preferences when it comes to using humor to communicate.

Important Note:
Learning to communicate can make one feel vulnerable, learning to communicate with humor, even more so. It's vital that we try not to be mocking, critical, accusatory or judgmental. It's too easy to fall into these negative mindsets. Instead, remember that each of us has an ongoing choice to approach one another with trust, love and laughter.

It's Important to Give Your Partner the Benefit of the Doubt

The first practical tip to help you use patience and humor in communication is to give your partner the *"Benefit of the Doubt."* Believe it or not, most pain inflicted in a relationship is *accidental.* Chances are, you're not married to a jerk. Giving someone the *"Benefit of the Doubt"* means, given all evidence to the contrary, you *first* assume that they did not mean to hurt you on purpose. This makes forgiveness far easier to offer because there's a lot less to forgive when you realize the behavior was accidental. If your wife snaps at you when she walks in the door at night, you *first* assume that she had a really bad day at work. If your husband didn't clean up the back yard after he said he would, you *first* assume that other important tasks came up and his intention was never to purposefully ignore your request. Giving your partner the *"Benefit of the Doubt"* allows you to avoid becoming immediately angry, and therefore, to potentially access your patience and humor - doing this can <u>dramatically</u> decrease the number of times a mere misunderstanding turns into full-scale conflict.

A "Moment of Grace" Helps One Communicate More Lovingly

Another practical tip on how to help each other with using patience and humor in communication is what I like to call a *"Moment of Grace."* Few of us will quickly master all of the communication skills we will be covering. So, when your partner blows it, (perhaps by saying something accidentally hurtful, or by not saying something you needed to hear, etc.), before you get angry, defensive and close down, hit that 5 second pause button and lovingly and kindly remind yourself and him/her of the new way you have agreed to communicate.

Offering this *"Moment of Grace"* gives your partner the chance to realize what's going on and the opportunity to get it right. For instance, if you start to tell your spouse something that hurt your feelings and they immediately jump to an offensive position, before becoming even more hurt and furious yourself, give them the *"Benefit of the Doubt"* and that *"Moment of Grace"* (therefore avoiding a damaging interaction) and say something like, "Sweetie, I'm sure you didn't mean to hurt my feelings, but remember this is one of the things that we're working on. Maybe we could try it the new way." In the end, it's easier to forgive someone for accidentally stepping on your foot than it is to forgive someone for intentionally stomping on your foot.

REAL LIFE EXAMPLE

Let me give you a more personal example of using all of these techniques. Recently, my husband was outside helping several kids safely take turns with a bow and arrow. The kids were a little rambunctious and I could tell he was starting to get frustrated. From the outside looking on, I could see what I thought was a far better and more efficient way to make this happen. I went outside and sweetly said, "Honey, can I speak to you?" He took one look at me and said just as sweetly, "Mmmm. No, I don't think so," and turned back to what he was doing. "What?!" I thought. I turned around and walked back into the house, very annoyed.

Back in the house, however, I remembered to give both him and myself the *"Benefit of the Doubt"* and a *"Moment of Grace."* I realized that what I was about to do was a little controlling (the man has known me for 20 years now – of course, he didn't want to talk to me!) However, I did still have some things I wanted to talk about, so a little later I went back outside. I could tell he was still a bit miffed at me. I walked over and said with a smile on my face and laughter in my voice, "Where exactly in the marriage manual, does it say you get to decline the 'Honey, can we talk' invitation?" He immediately smiled and responded with humor in his voice, "Oh yes, it's a little known clause; teeny-tiny writing. 'Husbands have the right to deny the 'Honey can we talk' question.' You must have missed it." By this time, we were both laughing out loud and had forgiven each other. The situation was completely diffused and we were able to have a loving and productive conversation about helping the kids with bows and arrows.

Love and Laughter
Further Communication

Can you think of any situations similar to the story above? Any recent issues that could have benefited with a little humor? When couples are able to give each other the *"Benefit of the Doubt"*, and that *"Moment of Grace,"* they are in a better position to forgive each other and approach each other with love and laughter. This goes a long way toward easing the situation and furthering their communication.

If you haven't done so already, now would be a good time to take our Marriage Success Quiz and find out if your marriage is setup to succeed for the long-term.
http://strongmarriagenow.com/successquiz

Exercise I1: Benefit of the Doubt

This exercise is designed to help you learn to give your partner the *"Benefit of the Doubt."* Remember, you're most likely not married to a complete jerk! There's almost always an alternative explanation for your partner's behavior. Truly understanding your partner's motivations leads to better communication and smoother conflict resolution.

Step 1: Write down the last time your partner made you mad.

_____

_____

_____

Example: *My husband was being distant and pouty when there was a change of plan with the kids' schedule and he couldn't get to the gym this weekend.*

Step 2: Write down what you thought was the motivation for their behavior at the time.

_____

_____

_____

Example: *I thought he was being stubborn and selfish.*

_____

Step 3: What else might explain their behavior? List some alternative explanations offering the *"Benefit of the Doubt:"*

_____

_____

_____

Example: *He was responding to the conversation we had the night before about taking better care of ourselves. He was feeling overwhelmed and needed some time to recharge. Changing directions in the middle of a plan makes him anxious.*

Exercise 12: Benefit of the Doubt

This exercise is designed to help you learn to give your partner the *"Benefit of the Doubt."* Remember, you're most likely not married to a complete jerk! There's almost always an alternative explanation for your partner's behavior. Truly understanding your partner's motivations leads to better communication and smoother conflict resolution.

Step 1: Write down the last time your partner made you mad.

_____

_____

_____

Example: *My husband was being distant and pouty when there was a change of plan with the kids' schedule and he couldn't get to the gym this weekend.*

Step 2: Write down what you thought was the motivation for their behavior at the time.

_____

_____

_____

Example: *I thought he was being stubborn and selfish.*

Step 3: What else might explain their behavior? List some alternative explanations offering the *"Benefit of the Doubt:"*

_____

_____

_____

Example: *He was responding to the conversation we had the night before about   taking better care of ourselves. He was feeling overwhelmed and needed some time to   recharge. Changing directions in the middle of a plan makes him anxious.*

What You Need To Know

1. It takes *time* to master communication skills.

2. The following principles make communication easier and more comfortable:

   a. Being patient with yourself and, more importantly, being patient with each other increases the likelihood that you will truly communicate and understand each other better.

   b. Making communication lighter and funny makes everything better and makes issues easier to solve.

   c. Being open and vulnerable brings down barriers to communication. Try not to be critical, accusatory, judgmental or respond like a victim.

   d. Giving your partner the "Benefit of the Doubt" is sometimes hard to do but essential to overall understanding. Remembering that most pain inflicted in a relationship is actually accidental makes it easier to forgive.

   e. Offering a *Moment of Grace* and the *Benefit of the Doubt* prevents one from jumping to the offensive or defensive position and gives your partner the opportunity to get it right.

Chapter 7

How to *Really* Listen

In this chapter, you will learn how to:

- Further deepen your connection
- Honor each other's feelings
- Get over long-standing issues
- Understand anger

One of the first things I talk about when helping couples with communication is actually the importance of *listening*. Most of us do fairly well when it comes to talking. Some people can even come up with charts, graphs and long lists of why they're "right," but they don't listen worth a darn. **Listening is, in fact, the most important part of communication in any relationship.** In the history of marriage, the ping-pong form of arguing, the back-and-forth of debate, has *never* resolved anything; until someone stops and listens, the match never ends.

There are 5 key points that will help you develop your listening skills as a couple.

- Listening is not the same as agreeing or obeying
- No issue is ever resolved until somebody genuinely listens and understands
- Everyone believes that their own feelings and opinions are right
- Anger is always the result of fear or pain
- Listening to each other deepens your connection as a couple

Listening is *Not* the Same as Agreeing

When most people say the words, "Listen to me," what they really mean is, "Agree with me!" How many times have you heard, "You're not listening to me!" When we hear this, we often interpret it to mean, "You're not agreeing with me!" and sometimes we're right; that is, in fact, what they meant. For those of us with children, when we say, "You're not listening to me," what we really mean is, "You're not obeying me." And trust me, our children know exactly what we really mean when we're saying it. So, the first thing we need to establish is that "listening" is *not* the same thing as agreeing, "hearing" is *not* the same thing as obeying, and "giving your spouse the opportunity to state their case," (without arguing or interrupting) is *not* the same as giving in to anything. Listening is, actually, just hearing and understanding what they are trying to tell you. That's it.

Nothing is *Ever* Resolved
Until Somebody Listens

Is there any topic that keeps coming up over and over again in your relationship? Is she still talking about that time you got too drunk back in college? Is he still talking about that time you talked to an old boyfriend? The reason for this is that the person who was hurt by the incident, never felt *truly heard* each time the topic was brought up. Over the *20 times* you may have already talked about it, somebody may have apologized repeatedly, explained themselves, even *promised* never to do it again. So why does it keep coming up? Because the person who is still bothered by it will continue to bring it up, **over and over,** until they feel like you *get it* — not necessarily agree with them --- but truly understand how they felt/feel about it. They are waiting for you to have that "A-ha" moment. And you can never have that "A-ha" moment if you don't listen.

Everyone Believes That Their
Own Feelings and Opinions Are "Right"

We should all know by now that everyone is entitled to their own feelings and opinions. We've all heard this, but what I am describing here is a little different. What I am saying is that every person genuinely believes that *their* feelings and opinions are absolutely correct and factual. So many arguments between couples are about who is "right" and who is "wrong." What they often don't realize is that in their own way, they are both "right," because everything they've experienced in life up to that point has led them to that opinion. Their opinion truly is, in that moment, *their reality*. The point of listening is for you to *understand* their reality. It's vitally important to give them the opportunity to explain why they believe what they believe and to listen.

Anger is Always the Result of Fear or Pain

It is also very important to keep in mind when you are attempting to listen to your partner that anger is a secondary emotion of fear or pain or both (remember that emotional broken arm from the chapter on "Forgiveness?") It is essential that you get this. Anger is *always* the result of fear or pain. If you're angry, you're hurt or scared or both, *every time*. This is a tough concept for couples. So, let me give you an example:

REAL LIFE EXAMPLE

Mary has asked Bob a thousand times to pick up his stuff around the house. Periodically, Mary blows up about this. Bob, understandably, reacts defensively and tells her to "quit nagging him." Now it's *on*. They engage in the traditional ping-pong match of arguing. When they come to see me, I ask Mary, what hurts and/or scares you about Bob not picking up his stuff? After some thought, Mary figures out that when Bob does not do what she asks, she feels like she's not important to him. Not only does that hurt her feelings, it scares her about the future of their marriage. Then I ask Bob, what hurts and/or scares *you* about Mary asking you to pick up your stuff? Typically, Bob responds with, "Nothing, it just pisses me off." After much resistance, Bob finally discovers that when Mary "nags" him, he feels like a failure because he truly does *not* remember or care about putting away his stuff and, therefore, feels hurt when he believes she sees him as a failure. Additionally, Bob *also* feels scared about the future of their marriage because to do it "her way," makes him feel controlled, "bossed" and backed into a corner. Once Bob and Mary understood the underlying feelings driving their anger, they were able to access some compassion for each other and listen to each other without feeling defensive. They were then able to forgive each other and work out a compromise that worked for them both.

Why is it important to know why your partner is hurt or scared? Well, when someone comes at you in anger, it's really easy to become defensive and come back at them with anger. However, when someone you love comes to you and says, "That really hurt me," or "This really scares me," that should be considerably more difficult to fight. So, here's the critical point of all of this – now *you* know that when *your* partner is angry, they are actually hurt or scared and that *should* matter to you. Have compassion for each other and really listen.

Listening to Each Other Deepens Your Connection as a Couple

We should always ask ourselves with each interaction, with each argument, even with each silence, "Is this bringing me closer or further away from the person I love?" Truly listening and making an effort to understand, (even when you agree to disagree), will always bring you closer. It helps you and your partner feel safe, understood and connected.

 **Exercise J1: Listening Exercise**

The point of this exercise is to try to *understand* the other person's point of view ---*not* to have a debate or even to reach an agreement. People cannot let go of or move forward from pain until they feel like you have had that "A-ha" moment and truly *understood* them. When a person feels *understood*, they are better able to trust and feel a deeper connection, which results in a stronger relationship.

Step 1: Choose who will be the Listener and who will be the Speaker.

Step 2: Review the rules and _prepare to follow them_.

Rules for both the Listener and the Speaker
1. Be patient - this is a difficult skill to learn.
2. Kindly help each other stay on track by **gently** reminding each other of the rules.
3. Set aside plenty of time. There are no time limits on this exercise. If the speaker needs to take 20 minutes to answer just one question, that's perfectly acceptable.
4. If the discussion becomes a back-and-forth debate or one of you has trouble following the rules, take a time-out. After that, review the rules, agree to follow them and resume the exercise.
5. A person may bring up the same topic as many times as they need to. Remember though, if this is happening, it's likely because the Speaker doesn't believe the Listener truly understands the Speaker's feelings.
6. When the exercise is over, it is over. Do not punish, pout or attack.

Rules for the Listener

1. Only ask questions.
2. Use a kind, sincere, and honestly-interested tone-of-voice.
3. Do not defend yourself, agree or even apologize during the exercise.
4. Do not debate "facts." For example, if the speaker says,*"You have not washed a dish in the last ten years!"* and you believe you have, simply nod and continue listening.
5. Do not show non-verbal cues or body language indicating you disagree. i.e. rolling your eyes, crossing your arms, looking angry, etc.
6. Do not construct your counterpoint argument in your head while the person is talking.
7. Do not ask leading questions such as: *"Don't you think I meant to do this?" "Can you imagine why I did that?"*
8. Do not answer questions posed by the speaker. If the speaker asks *"Why did you do that?"* Simply respond, *"This is about you, I just want to understand your perspective."*
9. Do not argue or share your side of the story when that person is done. Trust that your point of view will be heard at some point in the future.

Rules for the Speaker

1. Attempt to focus on one subject. For example don't say, *"It bothers me when you never do the dishes, like that time when your mother was here. I can't believe your mother is coming again! You always choose your mother over me, etc..."* Just say *"It bothers me when you never do the dishes."* and talk about that.
2. Do not attack. No name calling, no blows "below the belt" and no mocking.
3. Simply talk about your perception and feelings. You cannot feel a "that." (i.e. *"I feel that you are being a jerk."* is *not* a feeling.)

4. Be sensitive to how difficult this is for the Listener.

5. Do not ask questions - they cannot answer you.

Step 3: Speaker - Choose a topic.

When first learning this exercise, start off by choosing a topic that is relatively non-threatening:

Example topics:

- Leaving your clothes on the floor
- Focusing too much on the computer, TV and/or video games
- Not helping with the dishes
- Spending too much time with your friends
- Remembering a critical comment made last year

> *Note: Only bring up the really heavy topics after both the Listener and Speaker believe that they can consistently follow the rules.*

Step 4: Speak, Question and Listen

1. **Speaker** tells the listener the topic. "I want to talk about _____."

2. **Listener asks the following questions** about the topic chosen by the speaker. Do your best to stick to the questions below to keep the discussion on track. You can, however, feel free to ask clarifying questions to fully understand each answer. *i.e. "Tell me more." "Do you mean ____?"*

- "How do you feel about _____?"
- "Why do you feel that way?"

    (i.c. "What's underneath these feelings: your past, beliefs, culture, assumptions, etc.. ?")

- "What do you believe the intentions are/were?"
- "What do you wish happens/happened instead?"
- "Is there anything I can do to help?"
- "Is there anything that you believe I still don't understand?"

Step 5: Switch roles

When the new speaker chooses a topic, it must be a **new** topic. Do not rehash what was just discussed. Save your point of view on that topic for a later day.

Exercise J2: Listening Exercise

The point of this exercise is to try to *understand* the other person's point of view ---*not* to have a debate or even to reach an agreement. People cannot let go of or move forward from pain until they feel like you have had that "A-ha" moment and truly *understood* them. When a person feels *understood*, they are better able to trust and feel a deeper connection, which results in a stronger relationship.

Step 1: Choose who will be the Listener and who will be the Speaker.

Step 2: Review the rules and _prepare to follow them_.

Rules for both the Listener and the Speaker
1. Be patient - this is a difficult skill to learn.
2. Kindly help each other stay on track by **gently** reminding each other of the rules.
3. Set aside plenty of time. There are no time limits on this exercise. If the speaker needs to take 20 minutes to answer just one question, that's perfectly acceptable.
4. If the discussion becomes a back-and-forth debate or one of you has trouble following the rules, take a time-out. After that, review the rules, agree to follow them and resume the exercise.
5. A person may bring up the same topic as many times as they need to. Remember though, if this is happening, it's likely because the Speaker doesn't believe the Listener truly understands the Speaker's feelings.
6. When the exercise is over, it is over. Do not punish, pout or attack.

Rules for the Listener

1. Only ask questions.
2. Use a kind, sincere, and honestly-interested tone-of-voice.
3. Do not defend yourself, agree or even apologize during the exercise.
4. Do not debate "facts." For example, if the speaker says,"*You have not washed a dish in the last ten years!*" and you believe you have, simply nod and continue listening.
5. Do not show non-verbal cues or body language indicating you disagree. i.e. rolling your eyes, crossing your arms, looking angry, etc.
6. Do not construct your counterpoint argument in your head while the person is talking.
7. Do not ask leading questions such as: *"Don't you think I meant to do this?" "Can you imagine why I did that?"*
8. Do not answer questions posed by the speaker. If the speaker asks *"Why did you do that?"* Simply respond, *"This is about you, I just want to understand your perspective."*
9. Do not argue or share your side of the story when that person is done. Trust that your point of view will be heard at some point in the future.

Rules for the Speaker

1. Attempt to focus on one subject. For example don't say, *"It bothers me when you never do the dishes, like that time when your mother was here. I can't believe your mother is coming again! You always choose your mother over me, etc..."* Just say *"It bothers me when you never do the dishes."* and talk about that.
2. Do not attack. No name calling, no blows "below the belt" and no mocking.
3. Simply talk about your perception and feelings. You cannot feel a "that." (i.e. *"I feel that you are being a jerk."* is *not* a feeling.)

4. Be sensitive to how difficult this is for the Listener.
5. Do not ask questions - they cannot answer you.

Step 3: Speaker - Choose a topic.
When first learning this exercise, start off by choosing a topic that is relatively non-threatening:

Example topics:
- Leaving your clothes on the floor
- Focusing too much on the computer, TV and/or video games
- Not helping with the dishes
- Spending too much time with your friends
- Remembering a critical comment made last year

> *Note: Only bring up the really heavy topics after both the Listener and Speaker believe that they can consistently follow the rules.*

Step 4: Speak, Question and Listen

1. **Speaker** tells the listener the topic. "I want to talk about _____."

2. **Listener asks the following questions** about the topic chosen by the speaker. Do your best to stick to the questions below to keep the discussion on track. You can, however, feel free to ask clarifying questions to fully understand each answer. *i.e. "Tell me more." "Do you mean ____?"*

- "How do you feel about _____?"
- "Why do you feel that way?"

  (i.c. "What's underneath these feelings: your past, beliefs, culture, assumptions, etc.. ?")
- "What do you believe the intentions are/were?"
- "What do you wish happens/happened instead?"
- "Is there anything I can do to help?"
- "Is there anything that you believe I still don't understand?"

Step 5: Switch roles

When the new speaker chooses a topic, it must be a **new** topic. Do not rehash what was just discussed. Save your point of view on that topic for a later day.

What You Need To Know

Listening is the most important part of communication. It's also the skill with which most couples struggle.

1. Listening is not the same as agreeing or obeying.
2. No issue is ever completely resolved until someone genuinely listens.
3. Everyone's reality and feelings are their own and therefore feel "right" to them.
4. Anger is always a result of feeling fear or pain. If you're angry, you're hurt or scared or both - <u>every time</u>. Now you know that when your partner is angry, they are actually hurt or scared and that *should* matter to you.
5. Listening to each other deepens your connection as a couple.

What You Can Do To Understand Each Other

Here are the **Marriage Success System** *To-Do's* for this section:

1. **Offer forgiveness** and move forward.
2. **Get back in touch with your sense of humor** in order to lighten up conflict resolution.
3. Every time you're mad at your partner, attempt to **give him/her a** *"Moment of Grace"* **and the** *"Benefit of the Doubt."*
4. Each spouse: **practice the listening exercise** at least three times.

Be sure to go to Appendix B, cut out your Commitment Cards and post them where each of you will see them every day.

Section IV

Resolving Conflict

In this section, you're going to learn how to:

- Realize what's *really* going on and better communicate
- Prepare for and have a difficult conversation
- Resolve conflict in a healthier way and reduce damage from fighting
- Know yourself and your partner better

Chapter 8

How to Speak So Your Partner Hears You

In this chapter, you will learn how to:

- Have a clear purpose
- Say what's really going on (and not get side-tracked!)
- Talk about behavior and feelings
- Prepare for a difficult conversation

People take entire courses on how to speak effectively and I think it's a great idea if you've got the time. But I have found that there are really *three* key questions you should ask yourself when you are speaking with your partner:

1. What do I want to accomplish?
2. What do I need them to know?
3. What feeling/emotion am I trying to convey?

Connecting Should Be
the Main Goal

Begin by asking yourself "What do I want to accomplish?" The answer should always be that "I am trying to connect with my partner." Remember in the previous chapter on Listening, I wrote about each interaction bringing us closer together or further apart from our partner? This is what I meant: our primary goal should be to understand and to be understood, and therefore move closer to our partner. We often get so caught up in being "right," we lose sight of being unified and happy.

Thorough Communication Leads
to True Understanding

Next, ask yourself "What do I need them to know?" This is complicated because there are many parts to the answer. Many people jump right into what they think is the "solution."

    a. "Stop yelling at me!"
    b. "Aargh! Why don't you just call me when you say you're going to?!"
    c. "That's it! I'm never taking you to another work function!"

All of these are ineffective and often do more damage than good. They also lack other key information that, if thoroughly communicated, could help you be better understood and potentially decrease the chances of these painful situations happening again.

If you have an emotionally charged topic you need to communicate, the best way to get your point across is by using an "I" statement. An "I" statement is a technique to help better communicate difficult topics in a non-threatening way. There are four parts to an "I" statement. They look like this:

1. "I feel _____"
    a. "I *feel* hurt."
    b. "I *feel* rejected."
    c. "I *feel* embarrassed."

By beginning the statement with "I feel," you take responsibility for your own feelings. (On a side note, we cannot feel a "that." "I *feel* <u>that</u> you are being a jerk," is *not* an "I" statement.)

2. "when you _____"
    a. "I feel hurt when you raise your voice."
    b. "I feel rejected when you forget to call me."
    c. "I felt embarrassed when you criticized me in front of my boss."

State the specific behavior that caused the feeling. (Again, resist the temptation to make a judgment. Don't say, "I feel angry when you're annoying.")

3. "because_____"
   a. "I feel hurt when you raise your voice *because* it reminds me of my father."
   b. "I feel rejected when you forget to call me *because* it makes me feel unimportant."
   c. "I felt embarrassed when you criticized me in front of my boss *because* I worry he'll lose respect for me."

Explaining the consequences of the behavior helps the listener understand the impact of it.

4. "I'd appreciate it if you would_____"

This can be the most awkward part; guys in particular, often say it feels too touchy-feely, but it's extremely important. We often tell people what we *don't* want from them, but it's even more important to tell them what we *do* want. So go ahead and put it in your own words. Try something like:
   a. "I feel hurt when you raise your voice because it reminds me of my father. I'd rather you use a quieter voice when you speak to me."
   b. "I feel rejected when you forget to call me because it makes me feel unimportant. I'd appreciate if you didn't promise to call me if you're not sure you'll be able to."

c. "I felt embarrassed when you criticized me in front of my boss because I worry he'll lose respect for me. Please wait until we're alone to tell me something like that next time."

When you *kindly* and *lovingly* ask for what you need, it's so much easier for your partner to give it to you.

Tone of Voice Conveys Feelings More Than Words

Ask yourself "What feeling/emotion am I trying to convey?" This boils down to choosing the right tone of voice. In my practice, it sometimes surprises people when I explain that equally important to *what* we say is *how we say it*. In fact, sometimes it's *more* important. If I laugh and lightly say, "Ugh, you're seriously bugging me!" this has an entirely different meaning than if I glare at you and intensely say, "You are seriously bugging me." Same words but totally different tones of voice conveying totally different feelings. In fact, our voices can convey the entire range of emotions from humor, affection and patience to frustration, defensiveness and pain, (and sometimes do so without us even being aware of it....)

REAL LIFE EXAMPLE

Here's an example that brings all of this to life. I began seeing this couple who came to me to address their constant fighting over money. We'll call them Steve and Nancy. I quickly figured out that Steve and Nancy's biggest problem was, in fact, their poor communication, specifically *how* they spoke to each other. In other words, *what* they were trying to say to each other about money wasn't so bad. *How* they said it to each other was awful! Every time Nancy brought up her point of view, her tone of voice was blaming, condescending and totally shaming. She would say things to Steve in a snide and condescending tone of voice like, "You're so irresponsible, you don't care about our future. I guess *I'm* the only one that wants to buy a house." Nancy wasn't necessarily wrong about the need to save money and invest in a home for their family, but there was no way Steve was going to hear her when she spoke to him like that. When Steve replied, his tone of voice was cold and dismissive, effectively shutting down the conversation completely before anything could get resolved.

I asked Nancy, what she wanted to accomplish here?" She was quite clear on what she wanted to accomplish - she wanted him to admit that he was wrong, agree with her and do what she said! I reminded her that our number one goal in each interaction is not necessarily to be right, but to come closer together and get on the same page. She completely disagreed; she was right and he was wrong! This was their finances, their security, their future! I asked her again, do you want to be right or do you want to be happy?

While I know that money issues are important, her way of communicating about those issues was getting her exactly the opposite of what she wanted. Her approach wasn't going to get Steve to save money for the house; in fact, it just made him mad and more likely to spend it on the flat screen TV that made him feel better. I began teaching them about "I" statements and tone of voice. Once Nancy was able to remember her objective of being on the same page about money, she was able to speak to Steve in a way he could finally hear. She said in a calm and patient voice "I felt scared when you spent money on that flat screen TV because it meant we could put less into saving for a house. I'd appreciate it if we could make these decisions together in the future."

As you can imagine, after years of arguments over money, Steve was still shut down and initially still unwilling to hear her. I helped him work on his own "I" statement. It turns out that Steve didn't disagree with Nancy's opinions about money all that much at all, but was simply spending money to feel like he had some power over their finances. He made eye contact and quietly said, "I feel angry when you tell me how to spend money because it makes me feel controlled. I'd *also* appreciate it if we could make these decisions together."

When Steve and Nancy learned how to use "I" statements and remembered to use a kind and patient tone of voice with each other, they were able to finally come to agreements about money.

Asking these questions and using these techniques takes some time to become a habit. We might not get it perfectly right the first time (or even the seventh!). So please remember to offer the *Benefit of the Doubt* and that *Moment of Grace* that we discussed earlier as each of you asks yourselves:

1. What do I want to accomplish?
2. What do I need them to know?
3. What feeling/emotion do I want to convey?

Exercise K1: Preparing for a Difficult Conversation

Step 1: Ask yourself the following questions:

What do I want to accomplish in this conversation? *(Remember the primary goal is to connect)*

_____

_____

_____

What do I need him/her to know? *(Remember they'll hear this best with an "I" Statement)*

_____

_____

_____

What emotion/feeling do I want to convey? *(Remember anger is always a result of feeling fear and/or pain. Express the real emotion that is creating the anger)*

_____

_____

_____

Step 2: Prepare your "I" Statement.
This will help you communicate with your partner in a non-threatening way.

1. "I feel _____"
   (Take responsibility for your feelings)

2. "when you_____"
   (Describe the behavior or situation you'd like to address)

3. "because _____
   _____"
   (Share the consequences of the behavior and the impact that this has on you)

4. "I'd appreciate if you would_____
   _____
   _____."
   *(Ask **kindly and lovingly** for what you need)*

Here are some complete examples of "I" statements to help you prepare your own:

> *"I feel hurt when you raise your voice because it reminds me of my father. I'd appreciate it if you would use a quieter voice when you speak to me."*

> *"I feel rejected when you forget to call me because it makes me feel unimportant. I'd appreciate it if you would not promise to call me if you're not sure you'll be able to follow through."*

> *"I felt embarrassed when you criticized me in front of my boss because I worry he'll lose respect for me. I'd appreciate it if you would wait until we're alone to tell me something like that."*

Exercise K2: Preparing for a Difficult Conversation

Step 1: Ask yourself the following questions:

What do I want to accomplish in this conversation? *(Remember the primary goal is to connect)*

_____

_____

_____

What do I need him/her to know? *(Remember they'll hear this best with an "I" Statement)*

_____

_____

_____

What emotion/feeling do I want to convey? *(Remember anger is always a result of feeling fear and/or pain. Express the real emotion that is creating the anger)*

_____

_____

_____

Step 2: Prepare your "I" Statement.
This will help you communicate with your partner in a non-threatening way.

1. "I feel _____"
   (Take responsibility for your feelings)

2. "when you_____"
   (Describe the behavior or situation you'd like to address)

3. "because _____
   _____"
   (Share the consequences of the behavior and the impact that this has on you)

4. "I'd appreciate if you would_____
   _____
   _____."
   *(Ask **kindly and lovingly** for what you need)*

Here are some complete examples of "I" statements to help you prepare your own:

> *"I feel hurt when you raise your voice because it reminds me of my father. I'd appreciate it if you would use a quieter voice when you speak to me."*

> *"I feel rejected when you forget to call me because it makes me feel unimportant. I'd appreciate it if you would not promise to call me if you're not sure you'll be able to follow through."*

> *"I felt embarrassed when you criticized me in front of my boss because I worry he'll lose respect for me. I'd appreciate it if you would wait until we're alone to tell me something like that."*

What You Need To Know

1. There are three key questions you should ask yourself when you're speaking to your partner.

   a. **What do I want to accomplish?** This answer is always to connect. Don't be so focused on being right, that you lose sight of being united and happy.

   b. **What do I need them to know?** The best way to get your point across is with an "I" statement.

   c. **What feeling/emotion do I want to convey?** Use a kind, loving tone of voice.

2. It takes time to create a habit. Remember to offer the *"Benefit of the Doubt"* and a *"Moment of Grace"* (from the chapter on Patience and Humor).

Chapter 9

Fighting - What Not To Do

In this chapter, you will learn how to:

- Fight fairly
- Know your own triggers as well as those of your partner
- Gracefully resolve conflict
- Reduce damage from fighting

What's the first thing I'm going to tell you about fighting? Well, that's simple - Don't Fight. "What?!" you say. That's right! You can, (and will!), discuss, disagree, cajole, argue, persuade, differ, convince, entice, inveigle and (occasionally), bicker, but fighting is right out! Why, you ask? Well, we will be covering that in this chapter along with quite a bit more, including:

1. Fighting is <u>never</u> okay.
2. Know yourself and your partner.
3. Focus on the problem, not the person.

4. Find a way to compromise.

5. Gracefully accept a concession.

Fighting is Never Okay

One of the first things I tell my clients is that they should never *fight* again. They, of course, look at me like I'm crazy. I explain that the point of *fighting* is for someone to "win" and for someone to "lose" and that this only damages the relationship. So, as I mentioned above, we can discuss, argue, even vehemently make our point, but fighting is destructive and a complete waste of time.

Having said this, it is often difficult for people to let go of fighting because anger often feels good! It's a rush and feels invigorating. We feel in control. We feel righteous and safe, (safe from acknowledging our true feelings, that is). And we know from the chapter "How to Really Listen," that anger is always a result of feeling fear or pain, which are often far more complicated and uncomfortable to deal with. So if we're coming **at** each other with anger, it's most often because we're actually *not dealing* **with** our real emotions.

What I hear from people most often is "I can't help it! He makes me so mad!" What she clearly believes here is that she has no control over her emotions, that she simply "loses her temper." This is, in fact, rarely the case. I often ask if she has the same problem of "losing her temper" with her boss. "No," she replies, "I'd get fired." She usually starts to figure out where I'm going by this point. If one can control their emotions at the office, one can control their emotions with the most important relationship in their life. Our anger, like our mood, is *our choice*. It's not something that "happens" to us, it's something *we* create and fuel. Take responsibility for your anger and choose to *never fight again*.

If, in fact, you find that you truly can't control your temper, then there may be something else going on, like depression, substance abuse, or even a serious anger problem. If you think any of these might apply to you, I strongly encourage you to seek professional help today.

Avoiding Triggers Reduces Conflict

Everybody has "hot buttons." Those are the vulnerable spots each of us has that, when "pushed," make us completely crazy. It's extremely important to know our own and equally important to know what words or expressions tend to generate strong reactions from our partner. Learn them, respect them and, where possible, avoid them.

I call these triggers. These triggers are typically caused by painful and/or threatening experiences from the past and can cause you or your partner to strongly react. Knowing these triggers and avoiding them altogether can go a long way toward keeping your discussions pleasant and productive.

On a personal note, my trigger is the word "*Relax.*" Don't tell me to relax. Nothing makes me more instantly and irrationally irritated than to be told to relax. I find it dismissive and condescending. For my husband, however, don't roll your eyes. For whatever reason, based on everything that's happened to him before he married me, he reacts very negatively to eye-rolling. We know this about each other and respect it.

Every person has their own trigger words or behaviors that can make them instantly angry or unhappy. People react this way most often because these words or behaviors cause them to feel a real or perceived threat to their competence, worth, independence, or desire to be included.

Some of the most common triggers I hear in therapy are terms like "lazy," "controlling" or "bitchy." Many of these types of trigger words feel like name-calling to the person who hears them. Often the person saying them doesn't admit that they're name-calling because it's not technically profanity. But in actuality, any judgmental word we use to describe our partner is name-calling and unacceptable, period.

Now that you know the power and impact of triggers, talk to each other. Figure out what are your and your partner's "hot buttons" and do everything you can to respect and/or avoid them.

 # Exercise L1: Triggers

Painful and/or threatening experiences from the past can cause your partner to strongly react. Knowing these triggers and avoiding them altogether or dealing with them sensitively can go a long way toward keeping your relationship pleasant and comfortable.

Step 1: Reflect and identify your own triggers
(Examples: Being told to "relax," eye-rolling, being teased, being told what to do, being called certain names, being compared to others, leaving/walking away, certain tones of voice, etc.)

1. _____

2. _____

3. _____

Step 2: Identify their source
(These are typically from your childhood or painful experiences from the past)

1. _____

2. _____

3. _____

Step 3: Identify what you believe are your partner's triggers

1. _____

2. _____

3. _____

Step 4: Exchange exercises and discuss

Step 5: Triggers: Learn them, respect them and discuss better ways of dealing with them and/or avoid them altogether.

 ## Exercise L2: Triggers

Painful and/or threatening experiences from the past can cause your partner to strongly react. Knowing these triggers and avoiding them altogether or dealing with them sensitively can go a long way toward keeping your relationship pleasant and comfortable.

Step 1: Reflect and identify your own triggers
(Examples: Being told to "relax," eye-rolling, being teased, being told what to do, being called certain names, being compared to others, leaving/walking away, certain tones of voice, etc.)

1. _____

2. _____

3. _____

Step 2: Identify their source
(These are typically from your childhood or painful experiences from the past)

1. _____

2. _____

3. _____

Step 3: Identify what you believe are your partner's triggers

1. _____

2. _____

3. _____

Step 4: Exchange exercises and discuss

Step 5: Triggers: Learn them, respect them and discuss better ways of dealing with them and/or avoid them altogether.

Focusing on the Problem,
Not the Person, Leads to Solutions

Most arguments get off track by becoming personal and judgmental. In the chapter, "How To Speak So Your Partner Hears You," I shared an example about a wife criticizing her husband in front of his boss. Well, a lot of times that conversation ends up getting turned into a personal attack. "I can't believe you did that! You're so rude. You totally made me look like a total idiot!" Instead of focusing on the problem, the couple starts focusing on, and potentially attacking, each other.

Here's the problem. She criticized him in front of his boss. Instead of discussing that specific incident, most people come *at* each other until he or she crosses the line with a personal attack. The fight then becomes about that personal attack instead of whatever was the real issue in the first place. In other words, she instantly objects to "you're so rude" and he lobs back with "I'm not rude, you're just being a baby." And they're off. I tell couples that instead of fighting, they need to figuratively stand side-by-side and look at the problem together.

This is best achieved with a combination of "I" statements, the *"Benefit of the Doubt,"* and those *"Moments of Grace"* I keep talking about. They need to work as a team to find a solution, making the *problem* the issue, *not* each other.

In this particular example, she criticized him in front of his boss. They can come together and talk about what it felt like for him, what was going on for her, and how they both could handle it differently the next time. By doing this, they achieve the primary goal of *connecting* without wasting time on fighting. There should be no winner and loser when you're on the same team!

A Compromise is Mutual Acceptance

We've all heard this, right? But what most people think compromise means is meeting halfway, somewhere in the middle. The problem with this is that sometimes one person really does have the better idea. They may have more information, more experience or simply a better understanding of the situation and what needs to be accomplished. A compromise is actually *finding agreement through mutual acceptance*: presenting all of the available information that each of you has, understanding each other's points of view and then agreeing on a solution. Why that is so hard to accomplish brings us to our final point.

Gracefully Accepting a Concession Resolves Issues

Here, I am using the word concession to mean yielding, giving in, admitting we might be wrong. How many times have we been in the middle of a fight and realized the other person was in fact right, (or more right than we were anyway), but we kept fighting. This often has to do with pride, it sometimes has to do with *needing* to be right, but just as often it has to do with the *other* person's inability to gracefully accept a concession.

I don't know how many times I've heard one person in a couple say begrudgingly, "Well, you're right, I shouldn't have done that," only to have the other person respond with a triumphant gleam in their eye, "You bet I'm right! You never listen to me. Let me now tell you the other 27 times you've been wrong!"

I understand why people do this. They see it as an opportunity to increase their power in the relationship and they want to take advantage of that opportunity for as long as possible. Unfortunately, this just teaches their partner that it is not safe to *ever* admit they're wrong or to concede that their partner may have a valid point. And, chances are, if one person in the couple does not gracefully accept a concession, neither does the other one in an attempt to get that power back. This pattern effectively sets up a communication style that does not ever allow compromise or concession.

This is, in my opinion, one of the biggest barriers to resolving most conflicts in a relationship. It isn't that someone doesn't know they're wrong or that the other person is right, it's just that it's not safe to admit it.

Gracefully accepting a concession is not always easy, but it is very simple. Just say, "Thank you" or "I appreciate it," and move on.

Tying it All Together

Understanding Each Other and **Resolving Conflict** are both essential communication skills and are virtually impossible to master unless you follow the **Marriage Golden Rule**: "You must give what you want to receive in your marriage." Remember - if you want forgiveness, forgive. If you want the *"Benefit of the Doubt"* and a *"Moment of Grace,"* offer them. If you want to be heard, listen. If you don't want to be triggered, don't push your partner's buttons. If you want your apology to be accepted, gracefully accept concessions. And, if you want love and kindness, be loving and kind.

What You Need To Know

Always keep in mind the most important thing you need to know about fighting: Don't fight! Fighting is destructive and a complete waste of time.

1. **Fighting is never okay.** Our anger, like our mood, is our choice. Take responsibility for your anger and choose never to "fight" again.

2. **Know yourself and your partner.** Everybody has "hot buttons." Learn them, respect them and avoid them.

3. **Focus on the problem, not the person.** This is best achieved with "I statements."

4. **Find a way to compromise.** A compromise is *not* "giving in;" it is actually finding agreement through mutual acceptance.

5. **Gracefully accept a concession.** It's not always easy but it is very simple. Just say "Thank you or I appreciate it." and move on.

What You Can Do To Resolve Conflict

Here are the **Marriage Success System** *To-Do's* for this section:

- Prepare for and **have a difficult conversation** using "I Statements." Be sure to use the skills you learned earlier including: *"Moment of Grace," "Benefit of the Doubt,"* and Listening.

- If you have a disagreement, **step back and review the key skills** from the Fighting chapter and use them to resolve your issue.

- **Triggers--learn them, respect them and avoid them.**

Be sure to go to Appendix B, cut out your Commitment Cards and post them where each of you will see them every day.

Section V

Creating a "Marriage Plan"

In this section, you will learn:

- Why a "Marriage Plan" is needed for a successful future
- Why it's important to have a "Vision"
- Valuable tools to resolve conflicts around money
- How to have a Fair Division of Labor

Chapter 10

A "Marriage Plan"

In this chapter, you'll learn:

- How to create a "Marriage Plan"
- Why you need a "Vision" and how to create one

Now it's time to talk about money – an especially touchy subject, right? Yes, but an extremely important one. While most couples report that the number one area they want to improve in their marriage is communication, statistics actually show that money and/or an unfair division of labor are at the root of 70% of all divorces. Sometimes the impact of money is quite obvious:

> *"We're fighting all the time because she can't stop spending."*

> *"I only spend money because I have to do everything around here!"*

And, sometimes it's a bit more subtle:

> *"He's stressed and angry all the time because he hates his job, but can't leave it because we need the money."*

> *"She doesn't want to have sex anymore because she's exhausted from watching the kids all day and taking care of everything around the house, but we can't afford childcare or a housekeeper."*

Oftentimes these more subtle issues are further complicated by underlying resentment. For example: she secretly resents him for not making enough money or helping around the house and he secretly resents her for the constant nagging and reluctance to get a job.

Fighting Over Money Can Weaken Your Marriage

I don't believe money is the root of all evil, but it sure brings a lot of couples into my office! Constant fighting over money can taint even the strongest of marriages and can cause couples to lose sight of what is truly wonderful about their lives and wonderful about each other. So in this section, we're going to cover some basic strategies on how to effectively handle money; we're going to discuss and create what I like to call a "Marriage Plan." Many of you may know that to run a successful business: one needs a "Plan," a structured outline detailing the company's intended goals and how it proposes to reach those goals. Well, a successful marriage needs a similar kind of plan. This plan includes what I like to call a "Vision," a

"Budget" and "Job Descriptions." While these terms might sound intimidating to some people, agreeing upon them, and specifically, agreeing upon a Plan for the Marriage which encompasses all of them, can help a couple strive for the same goals and work together as a team to build the life they most desire.

Vision - Where Do you Want To Be in the Future?

When I refer to "Vision," I simply ask my clients this: Where do you see your marriage in one, ten, or even twenty-five years? Where do you see yourselves as a couple? As a family? You would be amazed at how many couples I see who have no idea how they would answer these questions, much less how their partner would answer them. Most often, they just vaguely assume that their partner feels exactly the same way that they do about their future together. And yet, they're frequently incorrect.

But, why does it matter if a couple is on the same page about their future? What difference does it make where we want to "end up?" Because where you want to end up, determines how you get there. In other words, knowing what the two of you want out of life, determines how you're

> "The future you see is the future you get."
> - *Robert G. Allen*

going to spend your resources, how you're going to invest your time and your money. And if the two of you are not on the same page about the Vision for the marriage, then you may be working at cross-purposes and threatening the very foundation of the marriage.

Finally, please understand that the Vision for the marriage will likely change over time. It's important to revisit and update your Vision over the years as your goals and desires evolve. And remember, this is virtually impossible to do unless you're spending quality time alone together.

> If you haven't done so already, now would be a good time to take our Marriage Success Quiz and find out if your marriage is setup to succeed for the long-term.
> http://strongmarriagenow.com/successquiz

Exercise M: Your Marriage Vision

This exercise will help you identify the Vision for your future. Understanding and agreeing upon the Vision will help you decide how you will spend your time and money. Sit across from each other and take turns answering the following questions. In the questions below, the word "where" does not refer to a place, but to a stage of life, including the state of your marriage, finances, social standing, relationships, etc.

1. Where do you see us as a couple in one year?

2. Where do you see us as a family in one year?

3. Where do you see us as a couple in ten years?

4. Where do you see us as a family in ten years?

5. Where do you see us as a couple in twenty-five years?

6. Where do you see us as a family in twenty -five years?

What You Need to Know

1. Constant fighting over money taints even the strongest marriages.

2. A successful marriage requires a Marriage Plan, which includes:

   a. Vision

   b. Budget

   c. Job Descriptions

3. Understanding and agreeing upon the Vision will help you decide how you will spend your time and money.

Chapter 11

Budget

In this chapter, you will learn:

- One of the easiest ways to solve money conflicts
- Why it's important to be *"Accountable to the Budget"* and not to each other

Now we can move on to the Budget. Most people usually flinch when they hear this word. It can often feel constrictive and limiting. But I encourage my clients to attempt to see it as the very answer to their money disputes. It's not that scary. The Budget is simply a mutually agreed upon outline of how much money is coming in and where it is, (or should be), going out. "Mutually agreed upon" being the most important part of this sentence: it rarely works for one partner to have the ultimate say over the couple's finances. Of all the sections in the Marriage Plan, this is the most important for a couple to put into place. Primarily because most fights about money are due to a difference of opinion about where the money should go and about who should have the ultimate say. These disagreements can result in a straightforward battle for ultimate control or in an ongoing seething resentment over the couple's financial situation.

Refer to the Budget
for Financial Decisions

So, I tell couples that instead of fighting each other about money, each party should be *"Accountable to the Budget."* In other words, when a financial decision needs to be made, refer to the Budget for permission, *not* to each other for permission. That's not to say that finances shouldn't frequently be discussed between the two of you, but not from a "parent/child" perspective. One partner should not have to ask the other for permission nor should the other partner believe they must give permission. Instead, the Budget becomes the "bad guy." If the Budget says we can't afford the new flat-screen TV, then we can be mad at the Budget, not at each other.

Budgets don't have to be complicated. Simply sit down and determine how much money is coming in and how much money is going out. After you know what's coming in, (after taxes), determine what you *have* to do. What are your day-to-day expenses and responsibilities, (i.e., food, bills, housing, etc.). Next, determine what you *want* to do, (i.e., paying off debts, saving for a house, college funds, retirement, etc.). Next, allocate funds in the Budget toward optional or discretionary expenses, (like entertainment, clothing, dining out, presents, etc.). Whatever is left after those three categories (have to do, want to do, optional or discretionary), we get to splurge or invest! Many couples have their spending priorities in the wrong order or they haven't thought about it at all, resulting in a constant state of worry, conflict, and denial over money. But there's no reason for that. If you want to know if you can afford something, ask the Budget! Taking the time to mutually agree upon, write down and follow your Budget can dramatically reduce a tremendous amount of stress and conflict.

REAL LIFE EXAMPLE Drew and Laila came to me for therapy to address what they called their "constant fighting." After just one session, I quickly determined that the prominent theme of almost all of their fights was money. Laila was hurt and resentful over the amount of time Drew spent working. She firmly believed that he cared more about his career than about her and the kids. She also believed that because he made more money, he believed he should have the ultimate control over their finances. Drew was also resentful and incredibly angry over the amount of money Laila spent. He said, "I only have to work this much to support the lifestyle she demands." Laila said, "He has no idea how much money it costs to run this house and family. Maybe he'd have a better idea if he was ever home." Both parties felt accountable to the other and seethed with righteous indignation.

Upon further investigation, it became apparent to all of us that despite the many "conversations" (fights) over money, neither one of them actually knew what was going on with the finances. Neither one had a Vision for their future, and there was certainly no Budget. When I suggested a Budget, Drew said, "It'll never work. We've had lots of Budgets, she's never followed them." She immediately bristled, believing that he would simply use the Budget as "another way of controlling" her. I explained to both of them that the Budgets had never worked in the past because they were not mutually agreed upon. They reluctantly agreed to give the Marriage Plan a shot.

It took a little while, (and a few sessions to work on improving their communication skills), but they finally arrived at a Marriage Plan. Laila felt empowered and invested; consequently she diligently followed the Plan. Drew was able to trust both Laila and the Budget and therefore, felt supported and financially safe, allowing him to work fewer hours. On a side note, eliminating the constant fighting over money allowed Drew and Laila to focus on what was great about their lives and helped them remember what they loved about each other.

I'm sure it will come as no surprise to you therefore, that the exercise for this chapter is to create a Budget. Again, don't get too complicated. Simply sit down and do the math. What's coming in and, based on your vision, where do you want it to go? Doing this will free you from the perpetual battles over money and allow you to invest in your relationship and in your future together.

Exercise N: Create Your Budget

Don't make this too complicated. If you don't know exactly what the numbers are, that's okay. You can go back to your checking account and credit card statements and paystubs for information or just estimate. It doesn't have to be exact to be very helpful.

Money that's coming in (Income)	Amount for the year
Income from work (after taxes)	
Income from investments (interest)	
Other income	
Total Income	
Money that's going out (Expenses)	
Day-to-day expenses (Have to Do)	
Housing	
Rent or mortgage	
Utilities (gas & electric, oil, water, etc.)	
Cable TV/Telephone	
Home Insurance	
Home Repairs	
Household items (dishes, furniture, etc)	
Other Home Expenses	
Vehicle Expenses	
Car Payment	
Gasoline/Fuel	
Car Insurance	
Other Vehicle Expenses	
Bills	
Credit card payments	
Student Loans	
Other bills	
Cell phone	
Food / Groceries	
Insurance (Life, Medical, etc.)	
Other Medical (co-pays, medicines, etc)	
Childcare	
Clothing	

Money for your goals (Want To Do's)	
Paying off debts	
Saving for a house	
College funds	
Saving for retirement	
Vacation fund	
Other goals	
Optional/Discretionary Expenses	
Entertainment (movies, music, etc)	
Entertainment (books, magazines, etc.)	
Misc Electronics (iPod, Video games, etc.)	
Dining out	
Gifts	
The latest fashions	
Other Discretionary Expenses	
Total Expenses (all three categories: Day-to-day expenses, Money for your goals and Optional/Discretionary expenses)	
I --Total Income (get total from above)	
E--Total Expenses (get total from above)	
What's left to re-budget, splurge or invest (Total Income – Total Expenses) (I– E)	

If you find that your total expenses exceed your total income, explore possible changes to be made in your situation either through modifying your lifestyle, or employment or financial compromises (e.g. moving, getting a room-mate, selling a car, turning off cable, etc.)

If your income exceeds your expenses, good for you! Now it's time to sit down and mutually agree upon where the surplus is going to go.

What You Need to Know

1. Having a Budget is a great way to reduce fighting over money

2. A Budget is a mutually agreed upon outline of how much money is coming in and how much is going out.

3. It's important to hold yourselves accountable to the Budget, *not* to each other.

4. In order, monies should be allocated to:

   a. Day-to-day expenses

   b. Your goals

   c. Optional/discretionary expenses.

   d. Fun and/or investments!

Chapter 12

Job Descriptions

In this chapter, you'll learn:

- The importance of specifying *"Job Descriptions"*
- How to clarify your expectations of each other
- How to better allocate responsibilities in your marriage
- How to create a "Fair Division of Labor"

The final part of the Marriage Plan is what I like to call "Job Descriptions." A company would never hire a new employee without first deciding and clearly delineating the expectations and responsibilities of that new position. Conversely, a job candidate wouldn't consider, much less accept, the job unless they fully understood what would be expected of them. Yet many couples march down the aisle having absolutely no idea what their role/job will be in their marriage (although they tend to have more than a few preconceived notions about the jobs of the person they're marrying!)

Job Descriptions Result in a Fair Division of Labor

Following money, this is the second most common reason couples fight (and they're very related). The two most common complaints I hear on this subject are: "I have to do everything around here." and "I am so tired of the constant nagging." What these couples need is an agreement on their Job Descriptions resulting in a Fair Division of Labor. A Fair Division of Labor is an equitable division of actual time spent on tasks that support the marriage and the family, including but not limited to: jobs, childcare, cooking, cleaning, chores inside and outside the home, doctors (and other) appointments, paying bills, purchasing household items, errands, home maintenance and repairs, phone calls, paperwork, entertaining, pet care, just to name a few.

There are many different ways that couples get confused about this issue. First, some attempt to handle it by demanding each chore be split in half, i.e., "I did the dishes yesterday, you do the dishes tonight." This rarely works as most people are good at, (or at least fine with), doing certain tasks. It is perfectly acceptable for him to be in charge of all cooking and her to be in charge of all electronic equipment maintenance.

The second mistake couples make is taking or giving ownership of certain areas without ever having discussed it. I can usually determine that this is occurring when I here something like, "You never *help* me with the kids," or "You never *help* me with the yard," as if to say that the kids or the yard are just one person's responsibility. As you can imagine, this leads to a skewed Division of Labor and can lead to significant resentment.

Fairly Dividing Responsibilities Can Reduce Conflict

Instead, I suggest that both parties list and agree upon all of the responsibilities it takes to effectively manage their marriage, their families and the household. (Exercise N: Job Descriptions). Once this list is created they can go about the task of fairly dividing the labor, time and energy required. This list now constitutes their Job Descriptions for the Marriage.

This exercise is often quite revealing and sheds light on a typical misunderstanding between the average working couple with kids. Let's say I, as a spouse, believe that there are around 100 things to do to run our lives. I further believe that I'm doing 75 of those, so you, by definition, can only be doing 25 of them. That seems unfair and it makes me angry. Well the good and bad news is this: after we sit down together and write out all that we take care of, we learn there are actually 150 things to do! Therefore, I *am* doing 75 things, but so are you. When couples figure this out, much of the resentment goes away and they are able to work through dividing those 150 tasks fairly.

Sometimes, however, the disproportionate division of labor is not an illusion and is, in fact, not fair. Current studies show that even in a household where both members of the couple have jobs, on average, the woman is still responsible for 80% of the household chores. However, this statistic can be misleading because it does not take into account the amount of time each person's job requires nor does it take into account the amount of time the husband spends caring for the children. It is, therefore, remarkably helpful to take an *actual* accounting of the amount of time each spouse invests in *all* aspects of maintaining the home and family. Writing down all tasks required to support the family, helps to illuminate to both spouses what needs to be done, and what each person is responsible for. Dividing these tasks more equitably, can reduce resentment and conflict tremendously.

Imbalances Are Usually Caused by Both Members of the Couple

Usually both members of the couple are at fault for this. Many men and women often take on too much of the responsibility due to their need to manage (dare I say, control) their environment. This often stems from their desire to appear capable and loving. Sometimes this stems from long-held beliefs of the definition of a good wife/husband and a good mother/father. Sometimes it is an inability, fueled by anxiety, to sit still. And, sometimes, it simply stems from the belief that if they don't do it, no one else will.

Men and women who take on less of the responsibility are often motivated by other priorities than marriage and kids, perhaps placing too much focus on their careers, hobbies or social lives. Additionally, it is almost always the case that the party who contributes less effort to the marriage, does not ever truly understand *all* that needs to be done.

Before I can wrap up this chapter, I need to talk frankly about a reality in which many couples find themselves. Sometimes each member of the couple has drastically different needs and expectations about what is required to care for the home and family. Some typical examples of this is are: the "slob married to the neat freak." the "hovering parent married to the *laissez-faire* parent" and to be brutally honest, "the self-absorbed person married to the giver." Arriving at a Fair Division of Labor for these couples requires utilizing *all* of the previous skills mentioned in this book, from learning to truly understand each other, resolving conflict, to compromising (arriving at a mutually agreed upon solution). The "slob married to the neat freak" must agree on a level of cleanliness and the means by which it will be attained, i.e. hiring a housekeeper or agreeing to clean together on Saturday mornings. The "hovering parent married to the *laissez-faire* parent" might agree to take a parenting course and to enforce those rules and boundaries for the children. The "self-absorbed person married to the giver" might seek education and mediation either through self-help books such as this, and/or counseling. When these types of differences occur, it's best to first determine how to handle these differences, and *then* work on the Job Descriptions.

Fortunately for most couples, determining a Fair Division of Labor and arriving at Job Descriptions is an easy issue to resolve. It's just simple math. There are 24 hours in a day and a certain number of things that need to be accomplished to make both members of the couple happy. The Job Description Exercise below provides an opportunity for each member of the couple to list what they believe are their current contributions of time and effort to the marriage and then arrive upon a Fair Division of Labor.

Exercise 01: Create Job Descriptions

This exercise will help you create Job Descriptions for your marriage. Having clear expectations of each other's tasks will help you agree on a Fair Division of Labor.

Step 1: List everything you do to support the household, how often it needs to be done and how long it takes:

Examples to include: jobs, childcare, cooking, cleaning, chores inside and outside the home, doctors (and other) appointments, paying bills, purchasing household items, errands, home maintenance and repairs, phone calls, paperwork, entertaining, pet care

What You Do	Time Per Week

Step 2: Now add up the time you spend per week to support the home:

Total Time: _____

Step 3: Gct together with your spouse and review each other's lists. If the Total Time appears unbalanced, agree to give-up or take on responsibilities until both parties are satisfied with their job descriptions.

Exercise 02: Create Job Descriptions

This exercise will help you create Job Descriptions for your marriage. Having clear expectations of each other's tasks will help you agree on a Fair Division of Labor.

Step 1: List everything you do to support the household, how often it needs to be done and how long it takes:

Examples to include: jobs, childcare, cooking, cleaning, chores inside and outside the home, doctors (and other) appointments, paying bills, purchasing household items, errands, home maintenance and repairs, phone calls, paperwork, entertaining, pet care

What You Do	Time Per Week

Step 2: Now add up the time you spend per week to support the home:

Total Time: _____

Step 3: Get together with your spouse and review each other's lists. If the Total Time appears unbalanced, agree to give-up or take on responsibilities until both parties are satisfied with their job descriptions.

What You Need to Know

1. An unfair Division of Labor is the second most common reason couples fight.

2. Both parties should list and agree on all of the responsibilities it takes to effectively manage their marriage, their families and their household.

3. On average, women are still responsible for 80% of household chores.

4. Both the man and woman in the couple are most often responsible for an unfair Division of Labor.

5. When couples have significantly different standards, they must first compromise and reach a solution. Then they can work on their Job Descriptions.

What You Can Do To Create Your "Marriage Plan"

Here are the **Marriage Success System** *To-Do's* for this section:

- **Review, discuss and agree on your Vision** for the marriage
- **Create a Budget** and get on the same page with your spouse about what funds are coming in and what is going out.
- **Complete the Job Description exercise** in order to have clearly delineated responsibilities in your marriage.
- **Review your Budget and Job Descriptions** once a month.

Be sure to go to Appendix B, cut out your Commitment Cards and post them where each of you will see them every day.

Section VI

All About Sex for the Couple

In this section, you're going to learn how to:

- Improve your sex life!

Chapter 13

Couples Guide to Sex

In this chapter, you will learn:

- How to get from "first base" to "home plate" more often
- That there's more to sex than intercourse
- To understand Mother Nature's "Big Joke"

I'm sure it comes as no surprise that one of the main issues that brings couples to therapy is disagreement around sex. A relationship is considered to have a problem with sex if *either* spouse is unhappy with the quality and/or quantity of sex. In this section, I'm going to talk about a lot of important concepts including:

- Viewing your relationship as a whole
- What I like to call "One of Mother Nature's Big Jokes"

- The significance of exploring the full range of sexual experiences
- The differences in men and women's arousal processes
- How feelings of excitement can change over time
- The importance of talking about sex
- How essential it is to start with a clean slate

Following this, there's a section tailored specifically for women and men, with a chapter dedicated to each of them separately. To ensure a well-rounded understanding of the subject, first read this Couple's Guide to Sex Section together. Then, read the Men's/Women's Guide to Sex Chapter that is tailored for each of you. As with all of our material, I am sharing a great deal of information with you. Feel free to stop, back up and read it again and again if you need to.

There are many different reasons why couples have difficulty in their sexual relationship. I have chosen to talk about the most common reasons -- the themes that come up in therapy time and time again. If these don't apply to you or if you find that the roles are, in fact, reversed, I still recommend reading these sections and then talking with your partner about which parts might apply to each of you.

It's Important to Understand One of Mother Nature's "Big Jokes"

Here it is! **A man feels connected** *by* **having sex. A woman needs to feel connected** *to want to* **have sex.** Neither one is wrong. But we often miss each other because we fail to understand this. I'll go into further depth about these differences in the individual chapters for men and women. For the purposes of this chapter, however, suffice it to say that sex for *both* partners is an attempt to achieve intimacy; they just take different paths to get to the same destination! Again, it's important to keep this in mind as you read the chapters on sex, because this is the cause of many misunderstandings around sex for both men and women.

There's a Whole Range of Sexual Experiences

The next important concept we need to define is sexual intimacy. People sometimes forget that there's a whole range of experiences between kissing and intercourse. All of this is sexual intimacy. Please understand that when I'm referring to sex in this material, I'm referring to anything within this range. Many couples, over the course of their relationship, lose touch with this range. This can be due to many different reasons including physical changes, such as weight, pregnancy, hormonal changes, etc. as well as relationship problems including poor communication, ongoing rejection, lack of affection, and basic discomfort around sexual issues. All of these can interfere with a couple's sex life. When this happens, couples can end up avoiding the whole thing rather than allowing themselves to explore the full range of intimate experiences. Therefore, in your conversations and explorations about sex, remember what most of us learned in high school: there's a whole heck of a lot of fun that can happen between kissing and actual intercourse.

Side Note:
If you have been experiencing some tension or issues around sex, starting lower on the range of these intimate experiences (i.e. kissing and snuggling), can help you connect again and feel safe as you explore your sexual feelings.0

Next, I'm going to talk about some major differences between a man and a woman's arousal process (and by process I mean getting from "first base" to "home plate!")

Understanding a Woman's Arousal Process

There are two main points that I want you to understand about the average woman's arousal process.

First, most women need to get *started* in the sexual process before they can even *begin to decide* if they want to have sex. Keeping our metaphor in mind then, this means that many women need to at least be "up to bat" or "rounding first base" before their minds and bodies let them know if they even want to finish the game. The problem is that women tend to wait to really *feel* like having sex before they even "step up to the plate." (Okay, the metaphor is getting old now - but you get the point...) One of the reasons for this is that most women don't feel safe starting something, if they're not sure they'll want to finish it. In other words, over time, many women stop giving passionate kisses to their husbands while standing in the kitchen because they feel horribly guilty if they get things started but don't end up having sex. This can develop into a pattern of avoidance. Many women even admit to picking fights and feigning the ever-famous headache just to avoid disappointing their husbands. Let me make that clear, they don't do it to avoid sex necessarily, they do it so that neither of them will have to feel the pain of a rejection.

How does this affect men? Well, one of the most common complaints I hear from men is, "The affection is missing. She doesn't touch me anymore; she doesn't kiss me anymore; she doesn't even want to hold my hand." Inevitably, I hear the woman say "Yeah, right. He just wants to have sex." She believes that if she starts with an affectionate kiss on the couch and doesn't take it any further, he'll be mad and she'll feel guilty. And often, she's right. Men can take this lack of follow-through very personally and can have a very negative reaction, so that it sometimes seems easier for both parties to avoid the whole thing.

So what can we do about it? We need to create an environment where the woman feels safe to step up to the plate regardless of whether or not she knows she wants to make it to home base. She should have room to be both affectionate and passionate. For this to work, however, she *also* needs to take some responsibility and be willing to engage in the process regardless of whether she already feels all hot and bothered. I'll get into this more in the Women's chapter. Finally, *both* partners need to be willing to ease up and not take the whole thing so personally. Sex should be fun! We have to lighten up! While we all hope to have the occasional mind-blowing marathon sex, (usually had on vacation with no kids), most married sex should be easy and light. We have to let go of the pressure - the pressure we put on ourselves and especially the pressure we put on our partners.

> Working on your sex life should
> feel like exploring the dessert buffet,
> not like choking down your
> least favorite vegetables.

Timing and Environment
Sets the Mood

The second thing to understand about a woman's arousal process is that it generally takes women a little bit longer to get engaged in the moment and get going. In today's world, people's minds are typically revving at high speed --- she may be thinking about work, the kids, chores around the house, what happened to a friend, etc. In order to slow down her mind and feel the sensations in her body, a woman needs time to make that happen and an environment free of distractions. By free of distractions, I mean, for most women, it's really hard to pay attention to the man of your dreams when you're looking at dirty clothes on the bed and kids toys on the floor. And speaking of setting the environment, *both* people need to remember to set the mood. One cannot criticize their partner about their job, their weight, how they made dinner, or how they treated the kids that night and expect them to feel willing to be vulnerable and eager to have sex.

Understanding a Man's Arousal Process

Most men usually have a much quicker arousal process. A glance, a touch, a kiss, can generally get him raring to go. Women, however, mistakenly assume that because it's quick, the feelings behind it aren't just as deep and meaningful. That's simply not true. A woman should not dismiss the depth of a man's feelings for her just because he can access them quicker than she can. Most men do think about their wife throughout the day and want to connect with her. And remember Mother Nature's "Big Joke," a man actually feels connected *by* having sex.

Make Love Throughout the Whole Day

So to wrap this point up, remember to flirt and stay connected throughout the day, put in the time to clear your mind and environment from distractions, then make it safe to just take it as far as it goes. Don't take it personally and lighten up! In other words:

> Make love throughout the whole day
> regardless of whether you
> end up in bed and chances are
> you'll end up there way more often!

Feelings of Excitement
Can Change Over Time

Now, let's get into how feelings of excitement can change over time. Many couples are unconsciously yearning for that amazing sensation, that rush they experienced in the first (roughly) two years of their relationship. And they feel that "something is missing" if it's not there. The bottom line is that you can't keep that going. I mean I could marry my favorite hot movie star tomorrow, (Hellooo, Mr. Depp!), and in about two years, when he walked in the room, I'd say in a loving yet benign voice, "Oh. Hi honey." His mere presence would no longer be enough to make me weak in the knees. Monogamy is, by definition, somewhat boring. It's not a natural state. You could be married to the best lover on the planet, but even champagne and caviar every day eventually gets dull. It's not personal and it doesn't mean that you're not still completely in love with your partner.

But, don't get discouraged! Because there are actual chemical and biological reasons for this, there are also ways to counter it. We *can* rev up those thrilling sensations. We *can* make it interesting and exciting again. How? By creating and putting ourselves in situations that are new, somewhat "risky," or even vaguely "forbidden." Whether that means taking up dancing, trying new positions, buying new toys, taking up white-water rafting or having sex on the beach! I'm just saying don't rely on the day-to day interactions to keep it interesting. Spice it up!

It's Critical To Talk To Each Other About Sex

None of the things I'm talking about can significantly improve, however, unless couples are communicating. I cannot emphasize enough how important it is to talk to each other about sex. A strange phenomenon occurs with many couples where they actually become *more* shy with each other over the years and find it incredibly difficult to talk about this very personal and intimate subject. They find it easier to do it than to speak about it! But they must talk about it. Couples often report to me that after spending several sessions discussing their fears and fantasies with each other, they are, in fact, amazed at how receptive their partner is. And that's how it should be.

Our spouse should be the one person on the planet with whom we feel safe exploring anything. And at the risk of repeating myself from a previous section, ...this takes time alone together.

Don't wait to talk about sex 'til you're in the bedroom. In fact, it's almost always a bad idea to talk about sexual concerns while you're in the bedroom. That doesn't mean that you can't provide encouraging suggestions now and again, you just want to avoid the heavy stuff while you're in the moment.

Wherever you are able to talk about it, however, it's imperative that you have *many* open and loving conversations about sex where you take what that other person says at face value. In other words, don't see your partner's sex life through your eyes. If she tells you, "I need dinner and a date before I really feel like the sex is about me," believe her. And if he says, "I don't feel like making love when you've just spent the last 20 minutes telling me how I can be better in this relationship," believe him. Many couples get frustrated in the therapy process because they report that they've repeatedly told their partner certain things over the years but, because their partners didn't feel the same way, they were never taken seriously.

Starting With A Clean Slate
Can Get You Back On Track

Another pattern that can get in the way of this "safe communication" is the final point I'm going to make in this chapter. Many couples have had a history of fighting about sex; they've made stupid comments that they now regret, they've rejected each other countless times for countless reasons and now have a wall that's built up between them. It's important for the two of you to start with a clean slate from here on out. Forgive each other for the mistakes you've made in the past and move on. (Refer to the chapter "Forgiveness and a New Beginning")

Thereafter, view your relationship as a whole, understand Mother Nature's "Big Joke," explore the full range of sexual experiences, respect the differences in men and women's arousal processes, remember how feelings of excitement change over time, and commit to talking about sex. If you do this, you will begin to look at your sex life as an opportunity full of possibilities, excitement and mutual satisfaction!

Exercise P1: Assess and Improve Your Sex Life

One of the most common reasons couples come to counseling is disagreements around sex. It's important to understand how both partners feel about the quality and/or quantity of sex they are having as well as to lovingly and openly discuss this often sensitive topic.

1. Grade your satisfaction with the QUALITY of your sex life
   1 - Extremely Satisfied
   2 - Satisfied
   3 - Neutral
   4 - Dissatisfied
   5 - Extremely Dissatisfied

2. Circle 2 things that would improve the QUALITY of your sex life
   - More excitement and enthusiasm
   - More variety
   - Less criticism or judgment
   - Meets more of my needs
   - More foreplay
   - More exploration of the whole range of sexual experiences
   - Increased sexiness
   - More exploration of fantasies
   - Increased trust
   - Other _____

3. Grade your satisfaction with the QUANTITY of your sex life

> 1 - Extremely Satisfied
> 2 - Satisfied
> 3 - Neutral
> 4 - Dissatisfied
> 5 - Extremely Dissatisfied

4. Circle 2 things that would improve the QUANTITY of your sex life

- More excitement and enthusiasm
- More variety
- Less criticism or judgment
- Meets more of my needs
- More foreplay
- More exploration of the whole range of sexual experiences
- Increased sexiness
- More exploration of fantasies
- Increased trust
- Other _____

5. Gently share your assessment with your partner.
Have a loving conversation. Choose one item from your partner's list and make it a priority to work on it.

Exercise P2: Assess and Improve Your Sex Life

One of the most common reasons couples come to counseling is disagreements around sex. It's important to understand how both partners feel about the quality and/or quantity of sex they are having as well as to lovingly and openly discuss this often sensitive topic.

1. Grade your satisfaction with the QUALITY of your sex life
- 1 - Extremely Satisfied
- 2 - Satisfied
- 3 - Neutral
- 4 - Dissatisfied
- 5 - Extremely Dissatisfied

2. Circle 2 things that would improve the QUALITY of your sex life
- More excitement and enthusiasm
- More variety
- Less criticism or judgment
- Meets more of my needs
- More foreplay
- More exploration of the whole range of sexual experiences
- Increased sexiness
- More exploration of fantasies
- Increased trust
- Other _____

3. Grade your satisfaction with the QUANTITY of your sex life

> 1 - Extremely Satisfied
> 2 - Satisfied
> 3 - Neutral
> 4 - Dissatisfied
> 5 - Extremely Dissatisfied

4. Circle 2 things that would improve the QUANTITY of your sex life

- More excitement and enthusiasm
- More variety
- Less criticism or judgment
- Meets more of my needs
- More foreplay
- More exploration of the whole range of sexual experiences
- Increased sexiness
- More exploration of fantasies
- Increased trust
- Other _____

5. Gently share your assessment with your partner.
Have a loving conversation. Choose one item from your partner's list and make it a priority to work on it.

What You Need To Know

1. The road to a good sex life requires constant intimacy to keep it on track. **View your relationship as a whole.**

    a. Remember to flirt and stay connected throughout the day.

2. **Understand one of Mother Nature's "Big Jokes."**

    a. A man feels connected by having sex. A woman needs to feel connected in order to want have sex.

3. There's a whole range of sexual experiences that can happen between "first base" and "home plate." **Explore the full range of sexual experiences.**

4. Men and women have different arousal processes. **Respect the differences.**

    a. Most women need to get started in the process before they can know if they want to go all the way.

    b. The depth of a man's feelings is not less simply because he can usually access his sexual feelings more quickly.

5. It helps to **lighten up** and not take the whole thing so personally.

6. **Feelings of excitement change over time.** After roughly two years, the thrilling sensation tapers off. To rev it up again, put yourselves in situations that are new, somewhat "risky," or even "forbidden."

7. If you don't **talk about great sex**, you won't have great sex. It's imperative that you have many open and loving conversations.

8. Couples can **start with a clean slate.** Forgive each other for the mistakes you've made in the past and start fresh.

What You Can Do To Improve Your Sex Life

Here are the **Marriage Success System** *To-Do's* for this section:

- **Talk to your partner** about what would improve the quality or quantity of your sex life (from Assess and Improve Your Sex Life Exercise).
- **Make an effort to stay connected** (flirt, call, compliment, etc.) throughout the day and week.
- **Lighten up** and start with a clean slate.

Be sure to go to Appendix B, cut out your Commitment Cards and post them where each of you will see them every day.

Section VII for Women

What You Can Do As A Woman To Improve Your Sex Life

In this section, you'll learn:

- How to keep your husband from straying
- Why women need to feel sexy
- How important sex is to a marriage
- What sex means to men
- The importance of a good attitude
- What to do when the roles are reversed

 **Chapter 14**

Women: Having the Right Attitude About Sex

In this chapter, you will learn:

- What sex means to men
- How essential it is to have the right attitude
- The importance of sex in a marriage
- How to keep your husband from straying

Ladies, I want to write to you individually because I've got some things to say that are sometimes hard for women to hear and in my typical fashion, I'm *not* going to sugar coat it for you. In this chapter, I'm going to cover the points that apply to most women. I understand that sometimes the roles are reversed but oftentimes this is due to the very same misconceptions I'm going to talk about here.

We're going to cover how men feel connected by having sex, the effect of positive thinking, the need to take responsibility for your own sexual feelings, why sex is important in a marriage, and how essential it is to make your man feel wanted.

A Man Feels Connected
By Having Sex

So, here we go, you've probably heard me say this before, but it's so important, I'm going to say it again: A woman has to feel connected in order to have sex: a man feels connected *by* having sex.

Why is that so important? It's important because men get a bad rap for wanting sex. I don't know how many times I've heard my female clients say, "He just wants to get laid. All he ever thinks about is sex." "Every time he touches me, he's just doing it because he wants sex." These statements are rarely true and almost always unfair.

So, let me explain how this works. Anyone who has ever been around little boys knows that they are very tactile creatures. From back scratches to rough-housing, they need to be touched to feel connected. That need never goes away. Men feel loved and connected by being touched. As men grow older, this need to be touched morphs into something sexual. But it amounts to the same thing. Sex makes men feel connected, appreciated, safe, and loved. And often women misunderstand this.

Thinking Positively Improves
Women's Sex Lives

Part of the reason women misunderstand this is due to the negative statements about sex that are often swimming around in their heads. We've heard them our whole lives, we say them to cach other and society supports these messages. I mean think about it. A woman *loses* her virginity but a guy *gets lucky*. Sitcoms make jokes about the women having to "give it up". And any female pop star who sings about wanting and actually liking sex is sending the "wrong message" to our little girls. And finally, many institutions, including some organized religions, give the message that sex for pleasure is evil or bad – mostly for women. So all of this is circling in our heads - then a woman becomes sexually active, and she's supposed to think sex is this amazing experience and a wonderful gift from God? This is often very confusing for most women.

So why are negative thoughts about sex and specifically one's own sexuality a problem? Well the problem is, as you may have heard, 80% of the sexual process for a woman happens in her head. So if many of our thoughts about sex are negative, we're going into it with an 80% handicap. A woman needs to get the *right* thoughts and attitudes about sex in her head. And here's the part that many of us don't want to hear. *That's our responsibility.* Only *we* can change our thoughts and attitudes.

It's also important to be around other women who have a good attitude about sex. What's the old joke? "A woman doesn't even have an orgasm until she tells her best friend about it." Being around women who have a good attitude about sex is great for your sex life! Being around women who complain about sex and their husbands is not good for your sex life --- or for your marriage for that matter.

Reducing Anxiety Can Improve Your Sex Life

On a deeper note, thinking positively about sex and having a good attitude about sex may be more complicated than we think as many women have developed an actual anxiety disorder around sex. They actually feel panicked when faced with the subject. Sometimes this stems from an early sexual trauma in one form or another and sometimes it is just caused by years of bad feelings surrounding sex. Some women create scenarios, go to bed early, start a fight or even fall asleep with the kids in order to avoid facing this issue. What you need to know, however, is this - anxiety is a condition that either lessens or increases every time we face it (or fail to face it). In other words, if one is afraid of heights, every time they step away from the cliff, that fear of heights grows, every time they step toward the cliff, that fear diminishes. Therefore, every time a woman's anxiety leads her to avoid having sex with her husband, it makes it even more difficult to get over the fear and have sex the next time. If this applies to you, it is *your* job to get closer to the edge. I encourage you to do whatever it takes to reduce these fears; apply the **Marriage Success Skills** taught in this book, write in a journal, talk to your girlfriends, even go to individual therapy if necessary. Do whatever you need to do to face your fears and move beyond them and closer to your husband.

A Woman's Sex Life is *Her* Responsibility

Women typically put too much of the responsibility for their feelings around sex on their men. Women often rely on men to make them feel beautiful, appreciated and sexy, rather than owning their part of getting their heads and their bodies (which we'll cover in the next chapter) in the right place. If you think about sex as a hassle and something you *have* to do, he can't change that for you. Only *you* can. I encourage you to take inventory of your thoughts around sex and replace any negative ones with positive ones. For instance,

> Rather than saying, *"Ugh, all he ever wants is sex."*
> Say, *"Aren't I lucky to have a husband who still finds me so desirable?"*

> Rather than saying *"He just wants to get off."*
> Say, *"Isn't it great that my husband wants to connect with me?"*

Be honest with yourself and *choose* to think positively about yourself, your husband and your sex life

---

Exercise Q: Re-frame Your Thoughts About Sex

The language that we use and the attitude we have toward sex dramatically effects how we approach it. Taking responsibility for your thoughts and feelings can significantly improve your sex life.

This exercise is designed to help you think more positively about yourself, your husband and your sexuality. These answers will be different for everyone. We've included examples to help you re-frame your thoughts.

1. How often does your husband want to have sex?

_____

i.e, *"All he wants to do is have sex."*

Re-frame:

_____

i.e, *"I'm so lucky that after all these years, he still finds me attractive and wants to have sex with and connect with me."*

2. How do you feel about your body?

_i.e,_ _"I feel so fat." "I hate my stomach."_

Re-frame:

_i.e,_ _"I'm so blessed to have a body that gave me my wonderful children. My husband still wants me so, clearly, he still thinks I look hot."_

3. How do you feel about your husband initiating sex?

_i.e,_ _"He's only being nice so he can get sex."_

Re-frame:

_i.e,_ _"How amazing that my husband attempts to meet my needs first so that we can connect and enjoy each other."_

4. What gets in the way of us connecting more often?

_i.e,_ _"If he would only _____, I would want to have more sex." "If the kids had gone to bed more easily, I'd be in a better mood." "I work all day, I take care of everyone, I'm exhausted."_

Re-frame:

_i.e,_ _"My sex life is my responsibility." "My mood is my choice. I'm going to let my stress go and connect with my husband"_

5. Do you enjoy sex?

_i.e,_ _"Sex is something I have to do, something I give in to doing." "Sex is a chore."_

Reframe:

_i.e,_ _"Sex brings me closer to my husband, makes him feel connected and strengthens our marriage."_

6. What in general are your thoughts on sex?

a._____

b._____

c._____

Reframe:

a._____

b._____

c._____

Sex is Vitally Important to a Marriage

But why does any of this matter? Why does sex matter? It matters because a relationship without sexual intimacy, by definition, is simply a friendship. And while we may truly love a friend, we are not "in love" with them. Sexual intimacy is what differentiates friends from lovers. It connects the couple on a deeper level, helps keep the marriage fun and exciting, and (if you're doing it right!), it creates a bond that you have with no one else on the planet.

A Sexually Satisfied Man Rarely Strays

Here's another one of those points that women typically don't like to hear. In 15 years of doing marriage counseling, I've never met a man who had an affair, who was satisfied with the sex life in his marriage. And by satisfied, I don't mean just regularly having sex; I mean, I've never seen a man want another woman when he felt his wife *really* wanted him. In a *Men's Health Magazine* Survey of married men, 50% of them rated their sex life as a grade C or lower. The top two things that all men who participated in the study wanted from their wives were increased initiation (they want you to go after them) and increased enthusiasm (they want you to be happy about it!) The bottom line, ladies, is that men simply want to be wanted. They need to know you're into *it* and into *them*.

Men Need to Feel Wanted

And not just into him when he's on his best behavior. Society, our mothers, our girlfriends have taught many of us to use sex as a reward for good behavior. Many women think that whether they feel sexual or not is dependent on everything around them, how he behaved that day, whether he did the dishes, whether he complimented her on her outfit, whether he watched the football game for too long, etc. So I'll say it again, women need to take responsibility for their own sexual feelings. We'd never have sex if it depended on our husband's being perfect. Nobody's perfect. (No, ladies, not even us.) Using sex as a reward teaches your man that it's something you're *willing* to do but not something you *want* to do. Be careful, because this leaves him vulnerable to someone who really *does* want him.

But what if the wife doesn't want him or want him very much? Let's be honest, sometimes women don't want to have sex because the sex isn't that great. This just brings me back to the point I made in the couples' section. It's extremely important to talk about sex, to figure out how you are satisfied sexually and then to ask for what you need. Most men want to please their women. They are just afraid to fail so they don't ask her what she needs.

> Figure out what works for you and *tell him*.
> You'll both have a lot more fun.

What You Need To Know - Women

1. **A man feels connected by having sex.** While women need to feel connected in order to have sex, just being touched helps your man feel connected, loved, safe and appreciated.

2. **Thinking positively about yourself, your husband and your sex life significantly improves the quality and quantity of sex.** 80% of sex for a woman occurs in her head.

3. Fear is a condition that lessens every time we overcome it or increases every time we avoid it. **Avoiding something we fear only increases our anxiety.** If this applies to you, do whatever it takes to overcome your fears and move closer to your husband.

4. **Your sex life is your responsibility.** It is not only our men's responsibility to make us feel beautiful, attractive and sexy.

5. **Sex is an important priority.** A marriage without sex is simply a friendship.

6. Men rarely stray when they are satisfied with the quantity and quality of sex in their marriage. **Make sure your man knows you want him.**

7. Most men want to please their women. **Figure out what you need and then tell him.**

Chapter 15

Women: Taking Care of Ourselves

In this chapter, you will learn:

- The importance of feeling sexy
- About medical issues that may be impacting your sex life
- How to deal with a low libido
- What to do when the roles are reversed

Taking Care of Yourself
Helps You Feel Sexy

Okay, yet another touchy point: If you want your husband to be attracted to you, you have to keep yourself attractive. This is different for different people. Some men like athletes and some men like curvy women.   But I'm not talking about weight or body type. What I'm really talking about is taking care of one's self. While I understand we all lead busy lives, wearing sweats every day with our hair in a ponytail and no makeup is not attractive to most men. And just as importantly, *we* don't feel particularly attractive like that. And if we don't feel attractive, we're simply not going to want to have sex. I'm not saying we have to dress up every day, but figure out how to put yourself together so that *you* feel sexy and *he* agrees.

Medical Issues Can Interfere With One's Sex Life

Sometimes however, the barrier to a great sex life is not in our heads, it's in our bodies. Many conditions from menopause, low testosterone levels, hypothyroidism, even some prescription birth control pills can dramatically reduce one's libido. If you truly believe your head is in the right place but your body is still not cooperating, see your doctor. Many of these conditions can be easily addressed and get you back on track to a great sex life.

If you determine that you do, in fact, have a low libido, you need to approach sex in a slightly different manner. Dr. Patricia Love, in her book Hot Monogamy, suggests that women with low sexual desire rarely experience earth-shattering sexual urges. For them, it's more like barely noticeable, mild tremors. Rather than waiting for the passion to sweep you off your feet, look for the more subtle signs: Do you think he looks good tonight? Do you like the way he smells? Did he just make you laugh? Did he just do something sweet for you? Or even, did the hot guy on the movie screen just put you in a slightly sexy mood? When any of these or other glimmers happen, build on them.

> "When you feel even the slightest pulse of desire, follow through with it."
> -- Dr. Patricia Love

Many Issues May be Occurring at Once

What can make the sexual process complicated, however, is that several of the issues we've discussed in the Women's section are frequently occurring all at once.

REAL LIFE EXAMPLE I saw a couple, Cindy and Jake, a couple in their early 40's, that had been married for over 10 years and had three young kids. In general, they got along pretty well. They loved their family, they loved each other, and their lives were basically comfortable. They came to therapy because Cindy's best friend's husband left her after having an affair and Cindy was growing progressively worried that this might happen to her marriage. Cindy's primary reason for feeling this way was that she and Jake were having sex *maybe* six times a year.

Like most couples, they didn't start out this way. They met after college, fell madly in love, got married and had awesome sex for the first few years. Babies started showing up, things started to wane and over the years they found themselves having very little sexual contact.

After several sessions, it turns out there were *many* contributing factors. As you can imagine, after three children, they had both gained a significant amount of weight. This gave Cindy great anxiety and she developed a pattern of avoidance that was maintained by negative thinking and reinforced by her girlfriends. After a few years of rejection, Jake gave up and took the attitude that if she wants me, she'll come get me. Cindy knew how important sex was, so she came to me. But what she came to me for, was to fix Jake so he would do all the "right" things to make her want to have sex again. As you can imagine, I didn't go for this. Don't get me wrong, Jake certainly had his part to play here, (most of which I cover in the men's section on sex). But since this is the women's section, let me tell you what Cindy learned.

She started taking better care of herself, which allowed her to feel sexier. She began paying attention to her body and acting on even the slightest impulse. She explored and overcame her discomfort with initiating sex and basically owned her part of the situation. On a side note, they also started spending 8 hours a week alone together and their sex life dramatically improved. Last I heard, they were both reporting satisfaction with both the quality and the quantity of their sex lives.

There May be Something Going on for Him

So, now I'd like to cover briefly when the roles are reversed. Every once in a while, I run into a woman who wants *way* more sex than her husband does. As you can imagine there can be many reasons for this. Many of them are similar to the ones we've covered here. He may feel uncomfortable with his body, *he* may have the lower libido, he may be experiencing a medical issue interfering with his ability to perform, or he may simply be feeling like he's not doing a good enough job pleasing you. Many men will avoid sex entirely rather than feel like a failure in bed. As you can imagine, this is an incredibly touchy issue. Most men are remarkably reluctant to talk about sex if they're the ones not having it.

In fact, talking to men about this will almost always shut them down. They rarely can be approached directly. If you determine that your husband is reluctant to talk about sex, first try going around the issue. If you suspect that he's uncomfortable with his weight, start including brisk walks in your date nights and family time together. If you're worried that he might have a medical problem, encourage him to get his yearly physical and pray that the doctor asks him the right questions. And if you get the impression that he's avoiding sex because he feels like a failure, go to great lengths to acknowledge his every success both in and out of the bedroom.

It Really Is About Quality Not Quantity

Finally, here's another point that women commonly just don't get. Most married men actually understand and accept that as time goes by the frequency of sex decreases. They're usually tired and overwhelmed, too! What really matters to them is the *quality* of the sexual encounter. (No, really, this is true!) Even if a couple has dropped their physical intimacies to every other week, in fact, *especially* if a couple has dropped to having sex every other week, they need to invest the energy to make it special. If the sex is satisfying to both of them, they both will feel more connected and happy.

Men Are Like Koalas

How do you know you're having good sex? Well, you know how men are on their best behavior when they *want* sex? They'll still be on their best behavior after having sex if the sex was good. Men are kind of like koala bears. Did you know that koalas are actually rather hyper, irritable creatures? However, there's a chemical in the eucalyptus leaves they eat that makes them perpetually mellow and happy. That's why they look all cuddly and sweet. Men are the same way and sex is their eucalyptus leaves!

Sex Shows Him You Love Him

So let me end with something I tell my female clients all the time.

> A woman should never have sex when she doesn't want to, but sometimes she should want to have sex because she loves him and it makes him feel good.

Most of the time we'll find that if we think positively, take responsibility for our own sexual feelings, remember how important sex is to the relationship, take care of ourselves, manage our own anxieties, and act on even our slightest sexual urges, we'll, (and he'll), be very happy we did!

What You Need To Know - Women

1. Feeling beautiful and sexy is *our* responsibility. **Take care of yourself.**

2. **Sometimes the barrier to a great sex life is in our bodies.** If you truly believe your head is in the right place, but your body is still not cooperating, see your doctor.

3. For women who have a low libido, noticing and **acting on even the slightest tremor or pulse of desire can help get them in the game.**

4. **Sometimes the roles are reversed.** If you suspect your partner is avoiding sex, first try going around the issue.

5. **Most men understand** decreased frequency as long as the quality is still high.

6. **It's okay to have sex just because you love him.** Men are like koala bears and sex is their eucalyptus leaf!

What You Can Do As a Woman To Improve Your Sex Life

Here are the **Marriage Success System** *To-Do's* for this section:

- **Keep your head in the right place.** Think positively about sex.
- **Put yourself together** so <u>you</u> feel confident and sexy.
- **Initiate sex** at least once.
- **Accept** your husband's sexual advances.

Be sure to go to Appendix B, cut out your Commitment Cards and post them where each of you will see them every day.

Section VII for Men

What You Can Do As a Man To Improve Your Sex Life

In this section, you'll learn:

- How a woman's mind works around sex
- How to turn your wife on and get her "in the game"
- Why power and control are sexy
- How to be irresistibly attractive to your wife
- What makes sex great for a couple

Chapter 16

Men: The Importance of Psychological Foreplay

In this chapter, you will learn:

- What sex means to women
- How a woman's mind works around sex
- How to get your wife "into the game"
- How to turn your wife on
- Why power and control are sexy

Welcome to the section What You Can Do As a Man To Improve Your Sex Life. This section is designed specifically for the man in the couple to read by himself. As you may have noticed, there is also a chapter designed specifically for women that outlines her role and responsibilities in the couple's sex life. Understand that my male clients usually hear this information over several weeks of once-a-week therapy sessions so it might seem overwhelming to read it all at once. But the beauty of this material is that you can review it at your own pace.

I want to address you gentlemen individually because I've got some things to say that are sometimes hard for men to hear and specifically sometimes hard for men to hear from a woman. What I'm going to tell you is based on years of research from the top experts in the fields of clinical and sexual psychology. Keep in mind that there is a lot of information here so take your time and try not to get overwhelmed. Not every point applies to every man. But I know how important sex is to a marriage so I want to give you as many keys as possible to unlock the full potential of your sex life.

Though it sometimes makes them uncomfortable, my male clients have consistently wanted to know what they could do to improve. So, I'm also going to share with you the information that they report has made the biggest impact on their sex lives.

I'll explain how the road to a good sex life is happening all of the time; that it's extremely important to invest in both the psychological and physical aspects of foreplay and that the individual issues that each partner struggles with are now the couple's issues together and tackling these together can lead to an exciting and satisfying sex life.

I'm going to cover how a woman needs to feel close to you and the importance of helping her keep her head in the right place. This will include: how essential it is for women to feel desired and how important it is for her to feel successful. We're also going to talk about the power and seductiveness of control and maturity.

She Needs to Feel
That She Matters

So let's get started. In the chapter, "Couples' Guide to Sex," I told you that a woman needs to feel connected in order to want to have sex, but what does "connected" mean? Well, the best definition I have come up with is simply, she needs to feel close to you; she needs to feel she *matters* to you. Also, in that chapter, I explained what the two of you can do to feel close to each other. We've talked about intimacy and that genuine intimacy requires time together, communication, shared experiences, vulnerability and openness with each other. Feel free to go back to the "Couples Guide to Sex" chapter to review these points. But now I need to tell you that there's more. If we're talking about what *you* can do to help, it all boils down to helping her consistently feel wanted, special, successful, safe, and attracted to you.

Whew! Sounds like a lot, right? In order for you to help her feel that way, we first need to talk about a common misunderstanding that I covered briefly in the couples' section:

> The road to a good sex life doesn't begin *five minutes* before you have sex.

Suffice it to say that men often complain to me in therapy that they are doing all of the things that I suggest, but they're not having any more sex. One client said to me, "After the kids went to bed, I asked her about her day and rubbed her feet, but that still didn't get us anywhere." Another client said, "We went out on date night. I told her she looked beautiful but when we got home, she turned me down again." This stems, interestingly enough, from a basic misunderstanding of foreplay.

Foreplay Creates Desire
for Sexual Activity

The dictionary defines foreplay as "a set of intimate psychological and physical acts between two people meant to create desire for sexual activity." In other words, the point of foreplay is to help someone *desire* sexual activity, it's not necessarily the activity itself.

Psychological Foreplay is
Happening All of the Time

So, let's pick this apart and start with the psychological aspect of foreplay. The most important thing we need to understand about this is that psychological foreplay is happening *all of the time.* I know this can sound terrifying to some men, but whether a woman ends up in bed, making mad passionate love that night, in large part depends on how she felt about her relationship with you, one hour earlier, that morning, and last week. But "why?" you ask. Well, as you may have heard: 80% of sex for a woman occurs in her head. If her head's not in the right place, her body can't get there either. As you can imagine, a woman's head is quite a complicated subject. In fact, I could do ten chapters explaining all the things you could do to help your wife get her head in the right place! But in the interest of time, I'm just going to cover the most common things you need to know to help you understand what to do.

Feeling Desired
Turns a Woman On

First, one of the primary things that psychologically turns a woman on is the feeling of being desired/wanted. There's a reason why the romance novel describing passionate love scenes in which the man is "burning with desire *for her*" is the number one selling genre of literature in the world.

Women need to believe that they are wanted and desired *specifically*, not just that their partners want to have sex with a woman in general. This is one of the most common complaints I hear from women in my practice. Many have actually said they simply feel like a vehicle for him to satisfy himself and that just doesn't turn them on. (In fact, it turns them off!) The men often counter this with the "But I have needs!" argument which actually makes the whole thing worse. Women interpret this statement to mean that their husbands have a "need" to have intercourse, but not a "need" or craving or desire for *her specifically*. Not only is this not enticing for a woman, it can actually feel rejecting. This is not to say that a woman can't enjoy sex just for sex's sake because she absolutely can, but in general, a woman needs to *feel desired* in order to *feel desirable*.

Make Sure She Knows
You Desire Her, *Specifically*

So what can a man do about it? Well, in the simplest of terms, he can attempt to make his wife feel like his desire for sex is about <u>her</u> - *her* body, *her* mind, *her* laugh, *her* sexy ankles! Just make sure she feels like the reason you want to make love has something to do with *her specifically*.

Side Note: One of the primary things that interferes with a woman feeling like she is wanted *specifically*, is when her man pays sexual attention to other women. Whether this is the age-old form of subtly checking another woman out, simply flirting with the waitress, or regularly looking at pornography. These seemingly harmless acts can dramatically effect how a woman feels about herself and more importantly effect how she believes *you* feel about her.

Feeling Successful
Turns a Woman On

The second thing that psychologically turns a woman on is feeling successful in her sex life. If she doesn't feel successful or, more importantly, if she feels like a failure, she tends to avoid it all together. So let's cover the most common ways men can make their wives feel like failures in the bedroom.

Making Passive-Aggressive Comments

Passive-aggressive behavior occurs when feelings of anger, (fear or pain), are expressed in indirect ways, such as intentional forgetfulness, stubbornness, withdrawal, sullenness, procrastination, or deliberate inefficiency. A passive-aggressive comment occurs when feelings of anger are indirectly communicated through sarcasm, negative teasing, or an "innocent" critical statement. Here are some examples: She's at a barbeque, flirts with her husband, implying he'll get lucky later. He jokingly says "Cool, I guess I did *something* right tonight," and everyone laughs. Or, she finally gets up the nerve to initiate sex and he laughingly says, "Wow, I love the *new* you." She sits next to him on the couch, leans in and he says "Oh good, we're going to sit on the *same* side of the couch tonight." And even after a particularly nice love-making session, he whispers in a sexy voice "Who are you and what have you done with my wife?" He's just joking, right? <u>Wrong</u>. All of these comments are meant to let his wife know he is unhappy with their regular sex life. They are embarrassing and shaming and they all make her feel like a failure. *Everybody* avoids activities that make them feel like a failure.

Avoiding passive-aggressive comments looks something like this: When she flirts with him at the BBQ, how about a sexy and mostly private wink from him, instead. When she initiates sex, he could say, "That was awesome." When she sits next to him on the couch, he could throw his arm around her and hug her close. And finally after a particularly nice love-making session, he could simply whisper, "I love you." All of these responses make her feel loved and *successful*, dramatically increasing the chances that she'll do all of these things again (and again, and again!)

Complaining and Blaming

But sometimes the comments aren't passive or subtle. Sometimes they are blatant and constant and even mean. I have seen many couples over the years that live with a constant pattern of complaints and avoidance. She will inevitably argue that she avoids sex because it's never enough, "He's never satisfied, so what's point?" He counters with "I only complain because she never wants to have sex." I understand how couples get in this rut and I have explained specifically what the women need to do about their part in this pattern in the women's section. But in this section, we're talking about *men* and I'm here to tell you nothing gets solved or improved in a relationship by constant blaming and complaining - *nothing* - not housework, not parenting, not finances, but *especially* not sex. In fact, openly complaining about sex will only get someone one thing: *less sex*. I mean think about it. Making someone feel bad about themselves or angry and defensive is exactly the opposite of where they need to be to want to have sex. I repeat, everybody avoids activities that make them feel like a failure. So instead, a man should consistently focus on the positive aspects of his wife, their marriage and their sexual relationship.

> A woman who is appreciated
> for even occasional sex
> will want to have it more often.

Appearing Disappointed

The third way a woman can end up feeling unsuccessful in her sex life is complicated to explain, but a very common occurrence. Everyone has probably heard that sex is a "use it or lose it" proposition. Well, the flip side of that is "the more sex you have, the more sex you want." That's great, right? A nice bonus from Mother Nature but, here's the complicated part: Women often end up feeling punished for having frequent and/or great sex because their partners are disappointed if the quality and/or quantity isn't somehow consistently maintained. In other words, after a great getaway weekend where a couple had several amazing lovemaking sessions, the couple have a big fight on Monday night when she's worked all day, unpacked, dealt with kids, cleaned the house, etc. and now just isn't in the mood. She goes to bed thinking it would have been easier if she had just kept it simple over the weekend and not made such an effort. This can set up a system where one or both members of the couple feels it's almost better to have mediocre and less frequent sex so that expectations don't get too high. The way to avoid this is to always focus on what you're *getting*, not what you're missing. Be grateful and at least appear satisfied with the night(s) you had great sex rather than putting the pressure on for a repeat performance. She'll feel good about herself and her sex life and want to get back to those feelings *much* sooner.

She Must Feel Safe

Additionally, I need to let you know that if any of these are occurring, the passive-aggressive comments, the constant complaining or the backlash for good sex, the woman does not feel safe in the sexual relationship and, as I'm sure you now know, feeling safe is one of the primary requirements a woman has to have in order to open herself up to a rich and passionate sex life.

One of the primary ways to avoid making these mistakes is to quite simply, not spend too much time with other people that make them. Don't play golf with a bunch of guys who bitch about their wives the entire time. Try to avoid socializing with other couples that make passive-aggressive and negative public comments about their sex lives. And above all else, do not listen to or commiserate with men, or people for that matter, who demean women, sex and marriage.

The Right Kind of
Power is Sexy

The next point we're going to discuss is something that men typically have the hardest time hearing, but it's a complaint I hear from women time and time again. Interestingly, it's almost always a complaint that women tell me privately. They instinctively know that their men don't want to discuss it, but I am committed to covering the most important things you need to know. So here we go...

Sexual excitement for a woman can largely be dependent on how powerful she views her partner to be. Women are attracted to power, but not always the kind of power one might think. So I'm going to tell you some things that women do and do not see as powerful.

Controlling *Yourself* is Powerful

First, women like a man in control; *I don't mean in control of her.* I mean a man **in control of** *himself*. A man who often loses his temper is not in control. A man who mishandles money is not in control. A man who sulks and pouts is not in control. A man who regularly loses his patience with the kids is not in control. A man who does not follow through on his commitments and responsibilities is not in control. A man who is constantly jealous is not in control. A man who drinks or parties too much is not in control.

Women interpret a man's losing control of himself as a weakness and **it's not sexy**. Additionally, if he is not in control of himself and his life, she feels like she has to be. This sets up a skewed power differential that leads women to feel like she has to be the "mother" in the relationship and that's not especially sexy to either one of them.

> A man who has control of *himself* elicits respect and respect is sexy.

Maturity is Hot

Second, women like maturity in the bedroom. While all of us love a guy who can be silly sometimes, woman also want to see their man as mature. By mature I mean able to approach sex from the point of view of an adult male, not a giggling, sixteen year-old, inexperienced kid. It's important that I really make the point here that I'm specifically talking about maturity *in the bedroom.* Women love a funny, lighthearted guy. It's one of the most attractive qualities in a man, in fact. But when transitioning into a more passionate place, women tend to be seduced by a man who is *serious* about his desire for her.

I had a couple in my practice that was having such difficulty in their sex life that he was considering ending their marriage. We worked on a lot of different aspects and things got a little better but they still weren't connecting very often. Finally, in an individual session with me she admitted what was really going on. She explained that while her husband was quite a powerful and successful man in both his business and family life, he got quite silly and uncomfortable when the topic of sex came up. Consequently, when they were alone, he used the language and made the moves of an immature adolescent. I can't tell you what a lot of that was. Suffice it to say that he approached sex like the awkward bumbling teenagers depicted in bad R-rated 80's movies. She said this had really always been the case, but it was getting worse the more problems they had in the bedroom. She tearfully explained that it really turned her off, but that she would never tell him for fear of hurting his feelings and his ego. I convinced her that at this point, she had nothing to lose by telling him. She reluctantly agreed. She told him privately and he was hurt and embarrassed, but he also quickly rallied and they were able to collaboratively come up with a new vibe that worked for both of them.

A lot of guys think this doesn't apply to them; they think, because the language or gesture is not a turn-off to them it must be fine. They also think everything's "fine" because their women don't tend to talk about it. I recommend that men pay attention to their wives faces and to the mood in the room. Sometimes things seem to be headed in the right direction and then there's a sudden shift or their woman shuts down. I recommend that guys pay attention to what was just said or done when the shift occurred. This can give them valuable insight. Because what I'm saying is this:

> While women do love guys who don't take themselves too seriously most of the time, in the bedroom, women are attracted to mature, confident, and assertive men.

"Nice" Guys Really
Do Finish First

Lastly and briefly, I need to say this. I know it sounds kind of obvious, but sexual activity is increased when the woman finds the man attractive. And by this I don't only mean physically attractive. Though a handsome face and great abs are nice, many women will tell you that some of the most "attractive" qualities in a man include a sense of humor, intelligence, being a great dad, a willingness to communicate and genuine kindness and compassion just to name a few. Working on and possessing many of these qualities can make a man powerfully attractive and downright irresistible!

Even a Few Changes Can
Make a Big Difference

So now you've heard the most important things I tell my male clients to help them improve their sex lives. Just keep in mind that they report that when they apply even a few of these skills, they see a *big* improvement.

Tying it All Together

So, to wrap up the psychological aspects of foreplay, remember the client's comment at the beginning about rubbing his wife's feet after putting the kids to bed and still not getting anywhere? Well, I found out what really happened. Yes, he rubbed her feet and asked her about her day, but he also had made an immature and premature grab at her chest that morning, lost his temper when he put the kids to bed, and made a passive-aggressive comment in the kitchen about finally getting lucky that night. Not surprisingly, she wasn't feeling all that into him. And the guy who didn't get anywhere after he took his wife out on a date? Yes, he told her she looked beautiful, but he also spent much of dinner working on his Blackberry, (and ignoring her), blatantly flirted with the waitress, and had blown off lunch with her parents the weekend before in order to go watch a game and drink way too much beer with his buddies.

Look guys, I told the women in the women's section that they make this way too complicated, and that they need to take responsibility for getting their bodies and their minds in the right place. But men have got to do their part, as well, by meeting them halfway. Once you know what you can do to help your wife get her head in the right place, you can both have more, (better!), sex.

> Help your wife feel connected, desired and
> wanted, and successful in her sex life.
> Seduce her by being a powerful man, by
> demonstrating control and maturity and your
> sex life will dramatically improve!

What You Need to Know

1. **A woman needs to feels connected in order to want to have sex.**

2. **The road to a good sex life is happening all of the time.** 80% of sex for a woman occurs in her head. Therefore, whether or not a woman wants to have sex depends on how she felt about her relationship an hour earlier, that morning and even last week!

3. **It's essential to invest in psychological foreplay.**
   a. A woman is turned on by feeling desired/wanted, *specifically*.
   b. A woman is turned on by feeling successful in her sex life. To help her feel successful:
      i. **Avoid making passive-aggressive comments.** Instead, make her feel successful and loved.
      ii. **Avoid constant complaining and blaming.** Instead, focus on the positive aspects of your wife and marriage.
      iii. **Avoid showing disappointment** if the quality and/or quantity of sex isn't maintained. Instead, be grateful and satisfied with what you're getting.

4. **A woman is turned on by power, control and maturity.**

Chapter 17

Men: How to Be Irresistible to Your Wife

In this chapter, you will learn:

- How to be irresistibly attractive to your wife
- What makes sex great for a couple
- How to dramatically improve your sex life

In this chapter, we're going to get into the physical aspects of foreplay including the importance of making the sex good for her and the role physical attractiveness plays in the relationship. We're also going to cover briefly why sometimes the roles are reversed.

A Little Education
Goes a Long Way

Discussing the physical aspects of foreplay is probably one of the most difficult subjects I'm going to cover in this book and another one of those things that most women are reluctant to tell their husbands, but here goes. Sometimes a woman doesn't want to have sex because the sex just isn't that good for her. Many couples have a very limited and predictable repertoire. Sometimes this is due to inexperience, but sometimes it's simply due to the nature of monogamy, which, as we mentioned before, can be somewhat boring. Usually, both members of the couple would like the sex to be better but neither one knows quite what to do about it.

Interestingly, men tend to be the ones most uncomfortable hearing what they could do to improve. Therefore, the first thing I encourage men to do is take responsibility and educate themselves. There are lots of good, legitimate sources of information about sex out there, including Dr. Patricia Love's book, <u>Hot Monogamy</u>, the tried and true Kama Sutra, and even the articles in Men's Health magazine, just to name a few. <u>Find some, read them, and apply them</u>. (Oh, and enjoy them!)

Secondly, I ask men to be brave, step out of their comfort zone and talk openly and honestly with their wife. Find out what she wants and needs to "get in the mood" and to be fulfilled. Accomplishing these two tasks will give you new, and hopefully exciting information that you can then apply in a capable and mature fashion - dramatically improving the quality and therefore the quantity of sexual experiences.

It Takes Time To Round All The Bases

While I'm not going to turn this into instructional reading on sexual technique, I do want to hit one of the most common tips that, when applied, can quickly improve a couples' sex life. I already covered, in the "Couples' Guide to Sex" chapter, how important it is for a woman to have enough time to get her head "in the game." Well, this directly applies to the physical aspect of foreplay as well. Remember foreplay helps a person get ready to have sex. So let me reiterate how important it is to invest the time to explore the *whole range* of sexual experiences from "first base" to "going all the way."

> Some men mistakenly focus
> too quickly on the "pink parts."

Women typically find foreplay and sex more satisfying when there's more time invested and the whole range of experiences is explored.

Women Are Attracted to a Man
Who Takes Care of Himself

Okay, this is another one of those sensitive issues. I told the women they need to take care of themselves and I'm going to tell you guys the same thing. Physical attractiveness truly doesn't matter as much to women, but it *does* matter. Women are attracted to a man who takes care of himself. And by taking care of himself, I mean physical fitness, grooming and presentation. Though it's a punch-line for many sitcom wives, the "holey underwear," the errant unwanted hairs and the ratty college t-shirts are simply *not* attractive. Learn what your wife likes to see you in and invest. But more importantly, a man should also take care of himself so that *he* feels attractive, confident and sexy. This in turn makes his wife feel the same way about him.

Exercise R: Help Your Wife Want To Have More Sex

This exercise is designed to help your wife feel more connected to you and therefore, want to have more sex with you.

Step 1: List all of the things you already do to help your wife know you love her, find her attractive (*specifically*), and appreciate her.

_____

_____

_____

_____

_____

_____

_____

_____

_____

_____

_____

_____

_____

_____

Step 2: Write 3 more things you can do to help your wife feel connected and attracted to you.

1. _____

2. _____

3. _____

Some examples:

1. Call her in the middle of the day
2. Kiss her when I walk in the door
3. Stay positive and supportive (stop complaining)
4. Tell her how much I appreciate everything she does
5. Don't lose my temper
6. Help maintain the home
7. Tell her she looks beautiful
8. Take control and handle issues powerfully
9. Stand up for her
10. Be a great dad
11. Make time for her
12. Make her a priority
13. Avoid paying attention to other women
14. Put myself together in a way I know she likes
15. Do an activity that she wants to do
16. Take her out on a date

Her Issues Are Now
The Couple's Issues

To be fair here I need to mention what many of you probably already know. Sometimes the lack of sexual interest on a woman's part is not due to attractiveness, poor technique or timing. Sometimes there's something actually physically or mentally going on with her. There are many times in a woman's life where her body naturally shuts down her sex drive: *e.g.* after having a baby, and menopause being the two most common. Additionally, she may have some psychological obstacles that were put in place long before she met her husband. But the bottom line is that her issues are now the couple's issues and she needs patience, support and participation to overcome them.

Sometimes the
Roles Are Reversed

Finally, we need to cover briefly when the roles are reversed. This is again one of those touchy subjects. But in some relationships, the roles are actually reversed and it is the woman who is wishing for more sex. This can occur for many reasons. Sometimes the man simply has the lower libido and naturally desires less sex. But oftentimes there are physical issues that interfere with a man's desire for sex. These include but are not limited to the effects of some medications, blood pressure problems, and weight gain. Sometimes there are psychological reasons like depression, anxiety or even ongoing extreme stress. And sometimes, it's due to the normal, natural aging process. If you feel that any of these apply to you, check with your physician.

All of our bodies change over time and they simply don't respond the way they did when we were 25 years old. Often men will avoid sex because they don't want to face or deal with one or more than one of these issues. I have seen lots of couples that had healthy, happy sex lives for many years but who, over time, dwindled down to a practically sexless marriage. Many times, this was due to the man's unwillingness to address one of these problems. Look, I know it can be difficult to talk to others about one's body, mind and sex-life but therapists and medical doctors are trained to help people address these issues and can really help. Take responsibility for yourself and take advantage of these resources.

Sex is Vitally Important to a Marriage

Finally, I want to say this, I understand that in our society, men often get a bad rap for wanting sex. And that's truly unfair and just not right. I know how important sex is to men and it is equally vital to a marriage, which is why I want to arm you with the information you need to have the sex life you both want! Enjoy!

What You Need to Know

1. To turn a woman on, it's essential to **invest in the physical aspects of foreplay.**

2. **It's important to make the sex good for her.** Take responsibility and get educated.

3. Invest the time to **explore the whole range of sexual experiences** from "first base" to "going all the way." *(Don't focus too quickly on the "pink parts".)*

4. **Women are attracted to men who take care of themselves.** Learn what your wife finds attractive and invest.

5. Sometimes the lack of sexual interest on a woman's part is due to actual physical or mental issues. **Individual issues are now the couple's issues to work out together.**

6. Sometimes the roles are reversed. Therapists and medical professionals are trained to address issues and can really help.

What You Can Do As a Man To Improve Your Sex Life

Here are the **Marriage Success System** *To-Do's* for this section:

1.   **Call her in the middle of the day**, ask her about how she's doing and *really* listen.

2.   **Kiss her** when you walk in the door.

3.   Do at least one thing to **help your wife feel successful** sexually.

4.   **Put yourself together** so you feel confident and sexy.

5.   **Make sure that sex is good for her.**

Be sure to go to Appendix B, cut out your Commitment Cards and post them where each of you will see them every day.

Section VIII

Ongoing Marriage Success

In this section, you're going to learn how to:

- Make Your Marriage Successful
- Use the **Marriage Success System** When You Need it
- Hold Yourself Accountable

Chapter 18

Our Sincere Hope For You

Congratulations, you've made it! Now you know what it takes to be happily married for the rest of your life. All that's left to do is to DO IT!

The **Marriage Success System** and this book are meant to be meaningful companions to your marriage; the skills taught within are to be applied by both partners on an ongoing basis. Continuing to consider and practice the skills you've learned here will keep your marriage vibrant and fulfilling.

> Be sure to take our Marriage Success Quiz periodically to regularly assess your marriage and monitor your progress so as to catch issues before they become big problems. Go to:
> http://strongmarriagenow.com/successquiz

If you find yourself returning to old habits or encountering new challenges, we encourage you to revisit the appropriate section; re-read it, carefully re-do the exercises and, once again, thoughtfully apply these skills to your relationship. We also encourage you to sign up for ongoing support and marriage advice at www.StrongMarriageNow.com.

As we have mentioned throughout this book, your marriage is your responsibility. It does not happen to you. You are not a victim of it; it is created by the two of you - you are your marriage. If the two of you are not happy in your marriage, it is because you have chosen not to be!

If you want to be happy in your relationship, *choose* to do whatever it takes, including but not limited to, following the ground rules, spending quality time alone together, learning to understand each other, effectively resolving conflict, agreeing on money, fairly dividing responsibilities, and having an awesome sex life.

We highly recommend that you do not wait for your partner to change first. It simply does not work. Instead, hold yourself accountable, try your best and stick with it.

Please remember that at one point in time, you considered your spouse to be your one true love, your beloved, and together you promised to stay true to each other forever. Surely, many of the qualities you fell in love with are still there. Take the time to remember what you're grateful for in your relationship, your family, and your life.

Our most sincere hope is for you to re-awaken those loving feelings and keep them alive for the rest of your days.

We wish you a lifetime of love and happiness!

Sincerely,
Dr. Dana and Amy
StrongMarriageNow.com

Acknowledgements

There are many people whose assistance and support have made this book possible. First, we'd like to thank Cara Fillmore for her invaluable contributions. Her tireless work of editing and refining the manuscript as well as her expertise with often humorous suggestions significantly enhanced this book.

We are exceptionally grateful to Sondra Modell Hirsch for her endless support and enthusiasm for the venture.

To our fantastic friends (you know who you are), thank you for all of your suggestions, participation, and motivating cheers. Without you guys, we wouldn't have been as energized and ready to surmount the challenges of such a daunting undertaking.

We also want to thank our clients and customers whose trust, feedback and personal experiences have truly brought this material to life.

To our amazing children, Aidan, Ryan, Jack & Kira, your laughs, hugs, kisses, (and willingness to entertain yourselves while we worked!) continue to remind us why we invest the time and effort to have great marriages and families. Thank you for being the fabulous beings you are.

And finally, we'd like to thank our husbands, whose unflagging support and encouragement helped our dreams become a reality. Their love and patience enabled us to found **StrongMarriageNow.com** and broaden our help of others while creating a successful business. We love you!

Dr. Dana and Amy

Appendix A: Marriage Success System Weekly Plan

Each "section" of this book corresponds to a week of the **Marriage Success System**. I recommend that couples follow this process to get the most out the material. Here is the Plan for the 7-Week **Marriage Success System** including what you will get out of each week:

Week 1: Getting Started. In this week, you'll learn about the **Marriage Success System** and how you can use it to dramatically improve your marriage. The System will help you:

- Agree on ground rules for working together during this process
- Remember why you chose each other in the first place
- Clarify what each of you wants from your relationship
- Take steps to start improving your marriage immediately

Week 2: Time. In this week, you will learn:

- The Secret of Happily Married Couples
- The *Most Important Lesson*

- How to better manage your priorities and balance your life
- How to "Make the Time"
- How to plan your Together Activities

Week 3: Understanding Each Other. In this week you're going to learn:

- How to forgive so you can move forward
- How to effectively apologize
- How to let go of the past and have a new beginning
- How humor makes everything easier
- The importance of giving your partner the *"Benefit of the Doubt"*
- How to honor each other's feelings and deepen your connection
- Why couples get stuck on long-standing issues

Week 4: Resolving Conflict. In this week you're going to learn how to:

- Realize what's *really* going on and better communicate
- Prepare for and have a difficult conversation

- Resolve conflict in a healthier way and reduce damage from fighting
- Know yourself and your partner better

Week 5: Creating a "Marriage Plan." In this week you're going to learn how to:

- Why a "Marriage Plan" is needed for a successful future
- Why it's important to have a "Vision"
- Valuable tools to resolve conflicts around money
- How to have a Fair Division of Labor

Week 6: All About Sex for the Couple. In this week, you'll learn how to:

- Improve your sex life!

Week 7 for Women: What you can do as an individual to improve your sex life. In this week, you'll learn:

- How to keep your husband from straying
- Why women need to feel sexy
- How important sex is to a marriage
- What sex means to men

- The importance of a good attitude
- What to do when the roles are reversed

Week 7 for Men: What you can do as an individual to improve your sex life. In this week, you'll learn:

- How a woman's mind works regarding sex
- How to turn your wife on and get her "in the game"
- Why power and control are sexy
- How to be irresistibly attractive to your wife
- What makes sex great for a couple

Appendix B: Weekly Commitment Cards

Week 1 - Section I - Getting Started:

Cut out and post these where each of you will see them every day:

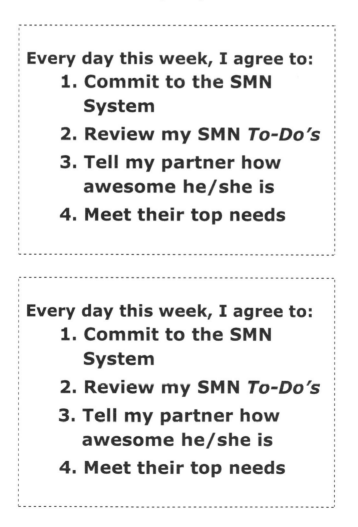

Every day this week, I agree to:
1. **Commit to the SMN System**
2. **Review my SMN *To-Do's***
3. **Tell my partner how awesome he/she is**
4. **Meet their top needs**

Every day this week, I agree to:
1. **Commit to the SMN System**
2. **Review my SMN *To-Do's***
3. **Tell my partner how awesome he/she is**
4. **Meet their top needs**

Every day this week, I agree to:
1. **Commit to the SMN System**
2. **Review my SMN *To-Do's***
3. **Tell my partner how awesome he/she is**
4. **Meet their top needs**

Every day this week, I agree to:
1. **Commit to the SMN System**
2. **Review my SMN To-Do's**
3. **Tell my partner how awesome he/she is**
4. **Meet their top needs**

Week 2 - Section II - Time:

Cut out and post these where each of you will see them every day:

Every day this week, I agree to:
1. Make my marriage #1
2. Schedule 8 hours of Time Alone Together
3. Choose and plan an "alone together" activity
4. Tell your partner how awesome he/she is
5. Meet another of their top needs

Every day this week, I agree to:
1. Make my marriage #1
2. Schedule 8 hours of Time Alone Together
3. Choose and plan an "alone together" activity
4. Tell your partner how awesome he/she is
5. Meet another of their top needs

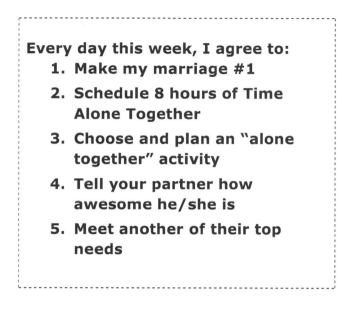

Every day this week, I agree to:
1. Make my marriage #1
2. Schedule 8 hours of Time Alone Together
3. Choose and plan an "alone together" activity
4. Tell your partner how awesome he/she is
5. Meet another of their top needs

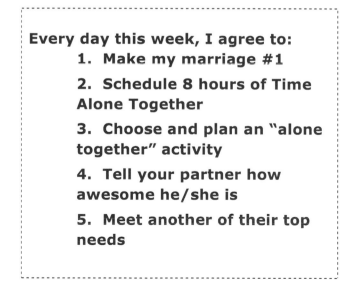

Every day this week, I agree to:
1. Make my marriage #1
2. Schedule 8 hours of Time Alone Together
3. Choose and plan an "alone together" activity
4. Tell your partner how awesome he/she is
5. Meet another of their top needs

Week 3- Section III - Understanding Each Other

Cut out and post these where each of you will see them every day:

Every day this week, I agree to:
1. Offer forgiveness and move forward
2. Get in touch with my sense of humor
3. Give my partner the "Benefit of the Doubt"
4. Really listen to my spouse

Every day this week, I agree to:
1. Offer forgiveness and move forward
2. Get in touch with my sense of humor
3. Give my partner the "Benefit of the Doubt"
4. Really listen to my spouse

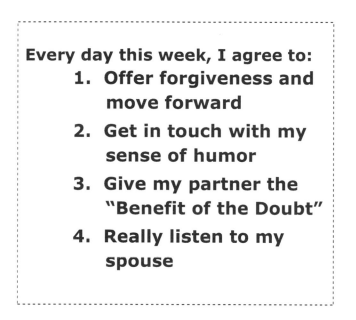

Every day this week, I agree to:
1. Offer forgiveness and move forward
2. Get in touch with my sense of humor
3. Give my partner the "Benefit of the Doubt"
4. Really listen to my spouse

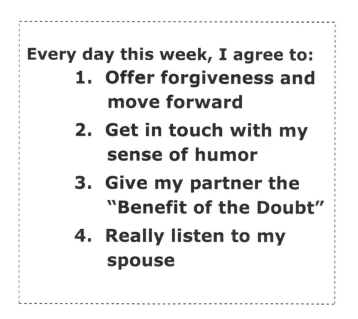

Every day this week, I agree to:
1. Offer forgiveness and move forward
2. Get in touch with my sense of humor
3. Give my partner the "Benefit of the Doubt"
4. Really listen to my spouse

Week 4 - Section IV - Resolving Conflict:

Cut out and post these where each of you will see them every day:

This week, I agree to:

> 1. **Prepare for and have a difficult conversation**
>
> 2. **Not fight**
>
> 3. **Learn, respect and avoid triggers**

This week, I agree to:

> 1. **Prepare for and have a difficult conversation**
>
> 2. **Not fight**
>
> 3. **Learn, respect and avoid triggers**

This week, I agree to:

1. Prepare for and have a difficult conversation

2. Not fight

3. Learn, respect and avoid triggers

This week, I agree to:

1. Prepare for and have a difficult conversation

2. Not fight

3. Learn, respect and avoid triggers

Week 5 - Section V – Creating Your "Marriage Plan:"

Cut out and post these where each of you will see them every day:

This week, I agree to:
1. Review, discuss and agree on your Vision 2. Create a Budget
3. Complete the Job Descriptions Exercise
4. Review our Job Descriptions together

This week, I agree to:
1. Review, discuss and agree on your Vision
2. Create a Budget
3. Complete the Job Descriptions Exercise
4. Review our Job Descriptions together

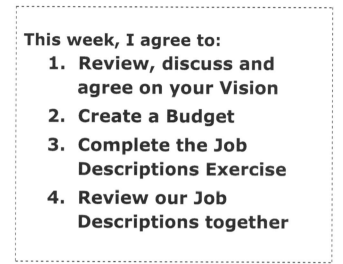

This week, I agree to:
1. Review, discuss and agree on your Vision
2. Create a Budget
3. Complete the Job Descriptions Exercise
4. Review our Job Descriptions together

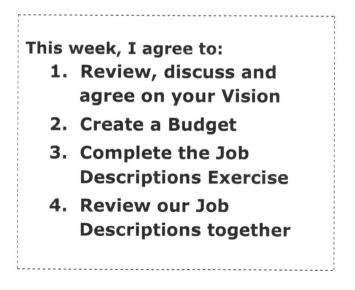

This week, I agree to:
1. Review, discuss and agree on your Vision
2. Create a Budget
3. Complete the Job Descriptions Exercise
4. Review our Job Descriptions together

Week 6 - Section VI – All About Sex for the Couple:

Cut out and post these where each of you will see them every day:

Every day this week, I agree to:
1. **Talk to my partner about sex**
2. **Make an effort to stay connected**
3. **Lighten up**

Every day this week, I agree to:
1. **Talk to my partner about sex**
2. **Make an effort to stay connected**
3. **Lighten up**

Every day this week, I agree to:
1. **Talk to my partner about sex**
2. **Make an effort to stay connected**
3. **Lighten up**

Every day this week, I agree to:
1. **Talk to my partner about sex**
2. **Make an effort to stay connected**
3. **Lighten up**

Week 7 - Section VII for Women: What You Can Do As An Individual To Improve Your Sex Life:

Cut out and post these where each of you will see them every day:

This week, I agree to:
1. **Think positively about sex**
2. **Put myself together**
3. **Initiate sex at least once**
4. **Say yes to my man!**

This week, I agree to:
1. **Think positively about sex**
2. **Put myself together**
3. **Initiate sex at least once**
4. **Say yes to my man!**

This week, I agree to:
1. **Think positively about sex**
2. **Put myself together**
3. **Initiate sex at least once**
4. **Say yes to my man!**

This week, I agree to:
1. **Think positively about sex**
2. **Put myself together**
3. **Initiate sex at least once**
4. **Say yes to my man!**

Week 7 - Section VII for Men: What You Can Do As An Individual To Improve Your Sex Life:

Cut out and post these where each of you will see them every day:

This week, I agree to:
1. Call her in the middle of the day every day
2. Kiss her each time I walk in the door
3. Do at least one thing to help my wife feel successful sexually
4. Initiate sex and make sure that it's good for her

This week, I agree to:
1. Call her in the middle of the day every day
2. Kiss her each time I walk in the door
3. Do at least one thing to help my wife feel successful sexually
4. Initiate sex and make sure that it's good for her

This week, I agree to:
1. Call her in the middle of the day every day
2. Kiss her each time I walk in the door
3. Do at least one thing to help my wife feel successful sexually
4. Initiate sex and make sure that it's good for her

This week, I agree to:
1. Call her in the middle of the day every day
2. Kiss her each time I walk in the door
3. Do at least one thing to help my wife feel successful sexually
4. Initiate sex and make sure that it's good for her

Appendix C: Online Resources

Please take advantage of our online resources to help you on your journey to a successful marriage.

Marriage Success Quiz

Happily Married or Headed for Divorce? Take the Marriage Success Quiz to find out where your marriage stands:

http://strongmarriagenow.com/successquiz

Free Marriage Success Secrets from Dr. Dana

Get FREE Marriage Success Secrets from Dr. Dana. You'll discover:

- The marriage truth no one ever told you
- The secret of happily married couples
- How to make everything easier in your relationship
- How to end the fighting
- Tips to improve your sex life

… and many more

Sign up today, go to:

http://strongmarriagenow.com/secrets

Marriage Success Solutions

To learn more about our StrongMarriageNow Marriage Success Products and Solutions to Revitalize Your Marriage, go to:

http://strongmarriagenow.com/solutions

About The Authors

Dr. Dana Fillmore

Dr. Dana Fillmore is a clinical psychologist, co-Founder of **StrongMarriageNow.com** and America's Leading Authority on Marriage Success.

Dr. Dana is known for being a clear, straightforward communicator who teaches the practical skills that couples need to be happily married for the long-term. She maintains, in fact, that because she and her husband regularly apply these Marriage Success Skills, they've weathered the ups and downs of marriage for over 16 years. She, her husband, her two kids and the dog are very happy together today.

Amy Barnhart

Amy Barnhart is the President & CEO of **StrongMarriageNow.com**. She began her career as an engineer and developed into a successful business executive. She has developed consumer products that millions of people love, including TurboTax ® and QuickenLoans ®.

Amy spearheads the technology, customer research and business side of StrongMarriageNow.com. Amy and her husband live in San Diego, California with their two children. They also regularly apply the Marriage Success Skills and have been happily married for 20 years.

Made in the USA
Lexington, KY
23 March 2013